No Treason

D1648974

By
Lysander Spooner

ANODOS BOOKS
Candida Casa

Lysander Spooner (1808–1887)
Originally published in 1867-70
Editing, cover, and internal design by Alisdair MacNoravaich for Anodos Books.
Copyright © 2018 Anodos Books. All rights reserved.

Anodos Books
1c Kings Road
Whithorn
Newton Stewart
Dumfries & Galloway
DG8 8PP

Contents

No Treason. No. 1.

I.

Notwithstanding all the proclamations we have made to mankind, within the last ninety years, that our government rested on consent, and that that was the only rightful basis on which any government could rest, the late war has practically demonstrated that our government rests upon force—as much so as any government that ever existed.

The North has thus virtually said to the world: It was all very well to prate of consent, so long as the objects to be accomplished were to liberate ourselves from our connexion with England, and also to coax a scattered and jealous people into a great national union; but now that those purposes have been accomplished, and the power of the North has become consolidated, it is sufficient for us—as for all governments —simply to say: *Our power is our right.*

In proportion to her wealth and population, the North has probably expended more money and blood to maintain her power over an unwilling people, than any other government ever did. And in her estimation, it is apparently the chief glory of her success, and an adequate compensation for all her own losses, and an ample justification for all her devastation and carnage of the South, that all pretence of any necessity for consent to the perpetuity or power of the government, is (as she thinks) forever expunged from the minds of the people. In short, the North exults beyond measure in the proof she has given, that a government, professedly resting on consent, will expend more life and treasure in crushing dissent, than any government, openly founded on force, has ever done.

And she claims that she has done all this in behalf of liberty! In behalf of free government! In behalf of the principle that government should rest on consent!

If the successors of Roger Williams, within a hundred years after their

State had been founded upon the principle of free religious toleration, and when the Baptists had become strong on the credit of that principle, had taken to burning heretics with a fury never before seen among men; and had they finally gloried in having thus suppressed all question of the truth of the State religion; and had they further claimed to have done all this in behalf of freedom of conscience, the inconsistency between profession and conduct would scarcely have been greater than that of the North, in carrying on such a war as she has done, to compel men to live under and support a government that they did not want; and in then claiming that she did it in behalf of the principle that government should rest on consent.

This astonishing absurdity and self-contradiction are to be accounted for only by supposing, either that the lusts of fame, and power, and money, have made her utterly blind to, or utterly reckless of, the inconsistency and enormity of her conduct; or that she has never even understood what was implied in a government's resting on consent. Perhaps this last explanation is the true one. In charity to human nature, it is to be hoped that it is.

II.

What, then, is implied in a government's resting on consent?

If it be said that the consent of the *strongest party,* in a nation, is all that is necessary to justify the establishment of a government that shall have authority over the weaker party, it may be answered that the most despotic governments in the world rest upon that very principle, viz: the consent of the strongest party. These governments are formed simply by the consent or agreement of the strongest party, that they will act in concert in subjecting the weaker party to their dominion. And the despotism, and tyranny, and injustice of these governments consist in that very fact. Or at least that is the first step in their tyranny; a necessary preliminary to all the oppressions that are to follow.

If it be said that the consent of the *most numerous party,* in a nation, is sufficient to justify the establishment of their power over the less numerous party, it may be answered:

First. That two men have no more natural right to exercise any kind of authority over one, than one has to exercise the same authority over two. A man's natural rights are his own, against the whole world; and any infringement of them is equally a crime, whether committed by one man, or by millions; whether committed by one man, calling

2

himself a robber, (or by any other name indicating his true character,) or by millions, calling themselves a government.

Second. It would be absurd for the most numerous party to talk of establishing a government over the less numerous party, unless the former were also the strongest, as well as the most numerous; for it is not to be supposed that the strongest party would ever submit to the rule of the weaker party, merely because the latter were the most numerous. And as matter of fact, it is perhaps never that governments are established by the most numerous party. They are usually, if not always, established by the less numerous party; their superior strength consisting in their superior wealth, intelligence, and ability to act in concert.

Third. Our Constitution does not profess to have been established simply by the majority; but by "the people;" the minority, as much as the majority.

Fourth. If our fathers, in 1776, had acknowledged the principle that a majority had the right to rule the minority, we should never have become a nation; for they were in a small minority, as compared with those who claimed the right to rule over them.

Fifth. Majorities, *as such,* afford no guarantees for justice. They are men of the same nature as minorities. They have the same passions for fame, power, and money, as minorities; and are liable and likely to be equally —perhaps more than equally, because more boldly—rapacious, tyrannical and unprincipled, if intrusted with power. There is no more reason, then, why a man should either sustain, or submit to, the rule of a majority, than of a minority. Majorities and minorities cannot rightfully be taken at all into account in deciding questions of justice. And all talk about them, in matters of government, is mere absurdity. Men are dunces for uniting to sustain any government, or any laws, *except those in which they are all agreed.* And nothing but force and fraud compel men to sustain any other. To say that majorities, as such, have a right to rule minorities, is equivalent to saying that minorities have, and ought to have, no rights, except such as majorities please to allow them.

Sixth. It is not improbable that many or most of the worst of governments—although established by force, and by a few, in the first place—come, in time, to be supported by a majority. But if they do, this majority is composed, in large part, of the most ignorant, superstitious, timid, dependent, servile, and corrupt portions of the people; of those who have been over-awed by the power, intelligence, wealth, and arrogance; of those who have been deceived by the frauds; and of those who have been corrupted by the inducements, of the few who really constitute the government. Such majorities, very likely, could be found in half, perhaps in nine-tenths, of all the countries on the globe. What do they prove? Nothing but the tyranny and corruption of the very governments that have reduced so large portions of the people to their present ignorance, servility, degradation, and corruption; an ignorance, servility, degradation, and corruption that are best illustrated in the simple fact that they *do* sustain the governments that have so oppressed, degraded, and corrupted them. They do nothing towards proving that the governments themselves are legitimate; or that they ought to be sustained, or even endured, by those who understand their true character. The mere fact, therefore, that a government chances to be sustained by a majority, of itself proves nothing that is necessary to be proved, in order to know whether such government should be sustained, or not.

Seventh. The principle that the majority have a right to rule the minority, practically resolves all government into a mere contest between two bodies of men, as to which of them shall be masters, and which of them slaves; a contest, that—however bloody—can, in the nature of things, never be finally closed, so long as man refuses to be a slave.

III.

But to say that the consent of either the strongest party, or the most numerous party, *in a nation,* is a sufficient justification for the establishment or maintenance of a government that shall control the whole nation, does not obviate the difficulty. The question still remains, how comes such a thing as "a nation" to exist? How do many millions of men, scattered over an extensive territory—each gifted by nature with individual freedom; required by the law of nature to call no man, or body of men, his masters; authorized by that law to seek his own happiness in his own way, to do what he will with himself and his property, so long as he does not trespass upon the equal liberty of others; authorized also, by that law, to defend his own rights, and redress his own wrongs; and to go to the assistance and defence of any of his fellow men who may be suffering any kind of injustice—how do many millions of such men *come to be a nation,* in the first place? How is it that each of them comes to be stripped of all his natural, God-given rights, and to be incorporated, compressed, compacted, and consolidated into a mass with other men, whom he never saw; with whom he has no contract; and towards many of whom he has no sentiments but fear, hatred, or contempt? How does he become subjected to the control of men like himself, who, by nature, had no authority over him; but who command him to do this, and forbid him to do that, as if they were his sovereigns, and he their subject; and as if their wills and their interests were the only standards of his duties and his rights; and who compel him to submission under peril of confiscation, imprisonment, and death?

Clearly all this is the work of force, or fraud, or both.

By what right, then, did *we* become "a nation?" By what right do we continue to be "a nation?" And by what right do either the strongest, or the most numerous, party, now existing within the territorial limits, called "The United States," claim that there really *is* such "a nation" as the United States? Certainly they are bound to show the rightful existence of "a nation," before they can claim, *on that ground,* that they themselves have a right to control it; to seize, for their purposes, so much of every man's property within it, as they may choose; and, at their discretion, to compel any man to risk his own life, or take the lives of other men, for the maintenance of their power.

To speak of either their numbers, or their strength, is not to the purpose. The question is by what *right* does the nation exist? And by what *right* are so many atrocities committed by its authority? or for its preservation?

The answer to this question must certainly be, that at least *such a nation* exists by no right whatever.

We are, therefore, driven to the acknowledgment that nations and governments, if they can rightfully exist at all, can exist only by consent.

IV.

The question, then, returns, What is implied in a government's resting on consent?

Manifestly this one thing (to say nothing of others) is necessarily implied in the idea of a government's resting on consent, viz: *the separate, individual consent of every man who is required to contribute, either by taxation or personal service, to the support of the government.* All this, or nothing, is necessarily implied, because one man's consent is

5

just as necessary as any other man's. If, for example, A claims that his consent is necessary to the establishment or maintenance of government, he thereby necessarily admits that B's and every other man's are equally necessary; because B's and every other man's rights are just as good as his own. On the other hand, if he denies that B's or any other particular man's consent is necessary, he thereby necessarily admits that neither his own, nor any other man's is necessary; and that government need not be founded on consent at all.

There is, therefore, no alternative but to say, either that the separate, individual consent of every man, *who is required to aid, in any way, in supporting the government,* is necessary, or that the consent of no one is necessary.

Clearly this individual consent is indispensable to the idea of treason; for if a man has never consented or agreed to support a government, he breaks no faith in refusing to support it. And if he makes war upon it, he does so as an open enemy, and not as a traitor—that is, as a betrayer, or treacherous friend.

All this, or nothing, was necessarily implied in the Declaration made in 1776. If the necessity for consent, then announced, was a sound principle in favor of three millions of men, it was an equally sound one in favor of three men, or of one man. If the principle was a sound one in behalf of men living on a separate continent, it was an equally sound one in behalf of a man living on a separate farm, or in a separate house.

Moreover, it was only as separate individuals, each acting for himself, and not as members of organized governments, that the three millions declared their consent to be necessary to their support of a government; and, at the same time, declared their dissent to the support of the British Crown. The governments, then existing in the Colonies, had no constitutional power, *as governments,* to declare the separation between England and America. On the contrary, those governments, *as governments,* were organized under charters from, and acknowledged allegiance to, the British Crown. Of course the British king never made it one of the chartered or constitutional powers of those governments, *as governments,* to absolve the people from their allegiance to himself. So far, therefore, as the Colonial Legislatures acted as revolutionists, they acted only as so many individual revolutionists, and not as constitutional legislatures. And their representatives at Philadelphia, who first declared Independence, were, in the eye of the constitutional law of that day, simply a committee of Revolutionists, and in no sense constitutional authorities, or the representatives of constitutional

6

authorities.

It was also, in the eye of the law, only as separate individuals, each acting for himself, and exercising simply his natural rights as an individual, that the people at large *assented to, and ratified the Declaration.*

It was also only as so many individuals, each acting for himself, and exercising simply his natural rights, that they revolutionized the *constitutional character* of their local governments, (so as to exclude the idea of allegiance to Great Britain); changing their forms only as and when their convenience dictated.

The whole Revolution, therefore, as a Revolution, was declared and accomplished by the people, acting separately as individuals, and exercising each his natural rights, and not by their governments in the exercise of their constitutional powers.

It was, therefore, as individuals, and only as individuals, each acting for himself alone, that they declared that their consent—that is, their individual consent, for each one could consent only for himself—was necessary to the creation or perpetuity of any government that they could rightfully be called on to support.

In the same way each declared, for himself, that his own will, pleasure, and discretion were the only authorities he had any occasion to consult, in determining whether he would any longer support the government under which he had always lived. And if this action of each individual were valid and rightful when he had so many other individuals to keep him company, it would have been, in the view of natural justice and right, equally valid and rightful, if he had taken the same step alone. He had the same natural right to take up arms alone to defend his own property against a single tax-gatherer, that he had to take up arms in company with three millions of others, to defend the property of all against an army of tax-gatherers.

Thus the whole Revolution turned upon, asserted, and, in theory, established, the right of each and every man, at his discretion, to release himself from the support of the government under which he had lived. And this principle was asserted, not as a right peculiar to themselves, or to that time, or as applicable only to the government then existing; but as a universal right of all men, at all times, and under all circumstances.

George the Third called our ancestors traitors for what they did at that time. But they were not traitors *in fact,* whatever he or his laws may have called them. They were not traitors in fact, because they betrayed nobody, and broke faith with nobody. They were his equals, owing him no allegiance, obedience, nor any other duty, except such as they owed to mankind at large. Their political relations with him had been purely voluntary. They had never pledged their faith to him that they would continue these relations any longer than it should please them to do so; and therefore they broke no faith in parting with him. They simply exercised their natural right of saying to him, and to the English people, that they were under no obligation to continue their political connexion with them, and that, for reasons of their own, they chose to dissolve it.

What was true of our ancestors, is true of revolutionists in general. The monarchs and governments, from whom they choose to separate, attempt to stigmatize them as traitors. But they are not traitors in fact; inasmuch as they betray, and break faith with, no one. Having pledged no faith, they break none. They are simply men, who, for reasons of their own—whether good or bad, wise or unwise, is immaterial— choose to exercise their natural right of dissolving their connexion with the governments under which they have lived. In doing this, they no more commit the crime of treason—which necessarily implies treachery, deceit, breach of faith—than a man commits treason when he chooses to leave a church, or any other voluntary association, with which he has been connected.

This principle was a true one in 1776. It is a true one now. It is the only one on which any rightful government can rest. It is the one on which the Constitution itself professes to rest. If it does not really rest on that basis, it has no right to exist; and it is the duty of every man to raise his hand against it.

If the men of the Revolution designed to incorporate in the Constitution the absurd ideas of allegiance and treason, which they had once repudiated, against which they had fought, and by which the world had been enslaved, they thereby established for themselves an indisputable claim to the disgust and detestation of all mankind.

In subsequent numbers, the author hopes to show that, under the principle of individual consent, the little government that mankind need, is not only practicable, but natural and easy; and that the Constitution of the United States authorizes no government, except one depending wholly on voluntary support.

No Treason. No. II.

THE CONSTITUTION says:

> "We, the people of the United States, in order to form a more perfect union, establish justice, insure domestic tranquility, provide for the common defence, promote the general welfare, and secure the blessings of liberty to ourselves and our posterity, do ordain and establish this Constitution for the United States of America."

The meaning of this is simply: We, the people of the United States, *acting freely and voluntarily as individuals, consent and agree* that we will coöperate with each other in sustaining such a government as is provided for in this Constitution.

The necessity for the consent of "the people" is implied in this declaration. *The whole authority of the Constitution rests upon it. If they did not consent, it was of no validity. Of course it had no validity, except as between those who actually consented.* No one's consent could be presumed against him, without his actual consent being given, any more than in the case of any other contract to pay money, or render service. And to make it binding upon any one, his signature, or other positive evidence of consent, was as necessary as in the case of any other contract. If the instrument meant to say that any of "the people of the United States" would be bound by it, who did not consent, it was a usurpation and a lie. The most that can be inferred from the form, "*We, the people,*" is, that the instrument *offered* membership to *all* "the people of the United States;" leaving it for them to accept or refuse it, at their pleasure.

The agreement is a simple one, like any other agreement. It is the same as one that should say: We, the people of the town of A—, agree to sustain a church, a school, a hospital, or a theatre, for ourselves and our children.

Such an agreement clearly could have no validity, except as between those who actually consented to it. If a portion only of "the people of the town of A—," should assent to this contract, and should then proceed to *compel* contributions of money or service from those who had not consented, they would be mere robbers; and would deserve to be treated as such.

Neither the conduct nor the rights of these signers would be improved at all by their saying to the dissenters: We offer you equal rights with ourselves, in the benefits of the church, school, hospital, or theatre, which we propose to establish, and equal voice in the control of it. It would be a sufficient answer for the others to say: We want no share in the benefits, and no voice in the control, of your institution; and will do nothing to support it.

The number who actually consented to the Constitution of the United States, at the first, was very small. Considered as the act of the whole people, the adoption of the Constitution was the merest farce and imposture, binding upon nobody.

The women, children, and blacks, of course, were not asked to give their consent. In addition to this, there were, in nearly or quite all the States, property qualifications that excluded probably one half, two thirds, or perhaps even three fourths, of the white male adults from the right of suffrage. And of those who were allowed that right, we know not how many exercised it.

Furthermore, those who originally agreed to the Constitution, could thereby bind nobody that should come after them. They could contract for nobody but themselves. They had no more natural right or power to make political contracts, binding upon succeeding generations, than they had to make marriage or business contracts binding upon them.

Still further. Even those who actually voted for the adoption of the Constitution, did not pledge their faith *for any specific time;* since no specific time was named, in the Constitution, during which the association should continue. It was, therefore, merely an association during pleasure; even as between the original parties to it. Still less, if possible, has it been any thing more than a merely voluntary association, during pleasure, between the succeeding generations, who have never gone through, as their fathers did, with so much even as any outward formality of adopting it, or of pledging their faith to support it. Such portions of them as pleased, and as the States permitted to vote, have only done enough, by voting and paying taxes, (and unlawfully and tyrannically extorting taxes from others,) to keep the government in operation for the time being. And this, in the view of the Constitution, they have done voluntarily, and because it was for their interest, or pleasure, and not because they were under any pledge or obligation to do it. Any one man, or any number of men, have had a perfect right, at any time, to refuse his or their further support; and nobody could rightfully object to his or their withdrawal.

There is no escape from these conclusions, if we say that the adoption of the Constitution was the act of the people, as individuals, and not of the States, as States. On the other hand, if we say that the adoption was the act of the States, as States, it necessarily follows that they had the right to secede at pleasure, inasmuch as they engaged for no specific time.

The consent, therefore, that has been given, whether by individuals, or by the States, has been, at most, only a consent for the time being; not an engagement for the future. In truth, in the case of individuals, their actual voting is not to be taken as proof of consent, *even for the time being.* On the contrary, it is to be considered that, without his consent having ever been asked, a man finds himself environed by a government that he cannot resist; a government that forces him to pay money, render service, and forego the exercise of many of his natural rights, under peril of weighty punishments. He sees, too, that other men practise this tyranny over him by the use of the ballot. He sees further that, if he will but use the ballot himself, he has some chance of relieving himself from this tyranny of others, by subjecting them to his own. In short, he finds himself, without his consent, so situated that, if he use the ballot, he may become a master; if he does not use it, he must become a slave. And he has no other alternative than these two. In self-defence, he attempts the former. His case is analogous to that of a man who has been forced into battle, where he must either kill others, or be killed himself. Because, to save his own life in battle, a man attempts to take the lives of his opponents, it is not to be inferred that the battle is one of his own choosing. Neither in contests with the ballot—which is a mere substitute for a bullet—because, as his only chance of self-preservation, a man uses a ballot, is it to be inferred that the contest is one into which he voluntarily entered; that he voluntarily set up all his own natural rights, as a stake against those of others, to be lost or won by the mere power of numbers. On the contrary, it is to be considered that, in an exigency, into which he had been forced by others, and in which no other means of self-defence offered, he, as a matter of necessity, used the only one that was left to him.

11

Doubtless the most miserable of men, under the most oppressive government in the world, if allowed the ballot, would use it, if they could see any chance of thereby ameliorating their condition. But it would not therefore be a legitimate inference that the government itself, that crushes them, was one which they had voluntarily set up, or ever consented to.

Therefore a man's voting under the Constitution of the United States, is not to be taken as evidence that he ever freely assented to the Constitution, *even for the time being.* Consequently we have no proof that any very large portion, even of the actual voters of the United States, ever really and voluntarily consented to the Constitution, *even for the time being.* Nor can we ever have such proof, until every man is left perfectly free to consent, or not, without thereby subjecting himself or his property to injury or trespass from others.

II.

The Constitution says:

> "Treason against the United States shall consist only in levying war against them, or in adhering to their enemies, giving them aid and comfort."

This is the only definition of treason given by the Constitution, and it is to be interpreted, like all other criminal laws, in the sense most favorable to liberty and justice. Consequently the treason here spoken of, must be held to be treason *in fact,* and not merely something that may have been falsely called by that name.

To determine, then, what is treason *in fact,* we are not to look to the codes of Kings, and Czars, and Kaisers, who maintain their power by force and fraud; who contemptuously call mankind their "subjects;" who claim to have a special license from Heaven to rule on earth; who teach that it is a religious duty of mankind to obey them; who bribe a servile and corrupt priesthood to impress these ideas upon the ignorant and superstitious; who spurn the idea that their authority is derived from, or dependent at all upon, the consent of their people; and who attempt to defame, by the false epithet of traitors, all who assert their own rights, and the rights of their fellow men, against such usurpations.

Instead of regarding this false and calumnious meaning of the word treason, we are to look at its true and legitimate meaning in our mother tongue; at its use in common life; and at what would necessarily be its true meaning in any other contracts, or articles of association, which men might voluntarily enter into with each other.

The true and legitimate meaning of the word *treason,* then, necessarily implies treachery, deceit, breach of faith. Without these, there can be no treason. A traitor is a betrayer—one who practices injury, *while professing friendship.* Benedict Arnold was a traitor, solely because, *while professing friendship for the American cause,* he attempted to injure it. An open enemy, however criminal in other respects, is no traitor.

Neither does a man, who has once been my friend, become a traitor by becoming an enemy, if before doing me an injury, he gives me fair warning that he has become an enemy; and if he makes no unfair use of any advantage which my confidence, in the time of our friendship, had placed in his power.

For example, our fathers—even if we were to admit them to have been wrong in other respects—certainly were not traitors *in fact, after* the fourth of July, 1776; since on that day they gave notice to the King of Great Britain that they repudiated his authority, and should wage war against him. And they made no unfair use of any advantages which his confidence had previously placed in their power.

It cannot be denied that, in the late war, the Southern people proved themselves to be open and avowed enemies, and not treacherous friends. It cannot be denied that they gave us fair warning that they would no longer be our political associates, but would, if need were, fight for a separation. It cannot be alleged that they made any unfair use of advantages which our confidence, in the time of our friendship, had placed in their power. Therefore they were not traitors in fact: and consequently not traitors within the meaning of the Constitution.

Furthermore, men are not traitors *in fact,* who take up arms against the government, *without having disavowed allegiance to it,* provided they do it, either to resist the usurpations of the government, *or to resist what they sincerely believe to be such usurpations.*

It is a maxim of law that there can be no crime without a criminal intent. And this maxim is as applicable to treason as to any other crime. For example, our fathers were not traitors in fact, for resisting the British Crown, *before* the fourth of July, 1776—that is, *before* they had thrown off allegiance to him—provided they *honestly believed* that they were simply defending their rights against his usurpations. Even if they were mistaken in their law, that mistake, if an innocent one, could not make them traitors in fact.

13

For the same reason, the Southern people, if they sincerely believed—as it has been extensively, if not generally, conceded, at the North, that they did—in the so-called constitutional theory of "State Rights," did not become traitors *in fact,* by acting upon it; and consequently not traitors within the meaning of the Constitution.

III.

The Constitution does not say *who* will become traitors, by "levying war against the United States, or adhering to their enemies, giving them aid and comfort."

It is, therefore, only by inference, or reasoning, that we can know *who* will become traitors by these acts.

Certainly if Englishmen, Frenchmen, Austrians, or Italians, making no professions of support or friendship to the United States, levy war against them, or adhere to their enemies, giving them aid and comfort, they do not thereby make themselves traitors, within the meaning of the Constitution; and why? Solely because they would not be traitors *in fact.* Making no professions of support or friendship, they would practice no treachery, deceit, or breach of faith. But if they should voluntarily enter either the civil or military service of the United States, and pledge fidelity to them, (*without* being naturalized,) and should then betray the trusts reposed in them, either by turning their guns against the United States, or by giving aid and comfort to their enemies, they would be traitors *in fact;* and therefore traitors within the meaning of the Constitution; and could be lawfully punished as such.

There is not, in the Constitution, a syllable that implies that persons, born within the territorial limits of the United States, have allegiance imposed upon them on account of their birth in the country, or that they will be judged by any different rule, on the subject of treason, than persons of foreign birth. And there is no power, in Congress, to add to, or alter, the language of the Constitution, on this point, so as to make it more comprehensive than it now is. Therefore treason in fact—that is, actual treachery, deceit, or breach of faith—must be shown in the case of a native of the United States, equally as in the case of a foreigner, before he can be said to be a traitor.

Congress have seen that the language of the Constitution was insufficient, *of itself,* to make a man a traitor—on the ground of birth in this country—who levies war against the United States, but practices no treachery, deceit, or breach of faith. They have, therefore—although they had no constitutional power to do so—apparently attempted to enlarge the language of the Constitution on this point. And they have enacted:

> "That if any person or persons, *owing allegiance to the United States of America,* shall levy war against them, or shall adhere to their enemies, giving them aid and comfort, * * * such person or persons shall be adjudged guilty of treason against the United States, and shall suffer death."— *Statute, April* 30, 1790, *Section* 1.

It would be a sufficient answer to this enactment to say that it is utterly unconstitutional, if its effect would be to make any man a traitor, who would not have been one under the language of the Constitution alone.

The whole pith of the act lies in the words, "*persons owing allegiance to the United States.*" But this language really leaves the question where it was before, for it does not attempt to show or declare who *does* "owe allegiance to the United States;" although those who passed the act, no doubt thought, or wished others to think, that allegiance was to be presumed (as is done under other governments) against all born in this country, (unless possibly slaves).

The Constitution itself, uses no such word as "allegiance," "sovereignty," "loyalty," "subject," or any other term, such as is used by other governments, to signify the services, fidelity, obedience, or other duty, which the people are assumed to owe to their government, regardless of their own will in the matter. As the Constitution professes to rest wholly on consent, no one can owe allegiance, service, obedience, or any other duty to it, or to the government created by it, except with his own consent.

The word *allegiance* comes from the Latin words *ad* and *ligo,* signifying *to bind to.* Thus a man under allegiance to a government, is a man *bound to it;* or bound to yield it support and fidelity. And governments, *founded otherwise than on consent,* hold that all persons born under them, are under allegiance to them; that is, are bound to render them support, fidelity, and obedience; and are traitors if they resist them.

But it is obvious that, *in truth and in fact,* no one but himself can bind any one to support any government. And our Constitution admits this fact when it concedes that it derives its authority wholly from the consent of the people. And the word treason is to be understood in accordance with that idea.

15

It is conceded that a person of foreign birth comes under allegiance to our government only by special voluntary contract. If a native has allegiance imposed upon him, against his will, he is in a worse condition than the foreigner; for the latter can do as he pleases about assuming that obligation. The accepted interpretation of the Constitution, therefore, makes the foreigner a free person, on this point, while it makes the native a slave.

The only difference—*if there be any*—between natives and foreigners, in respect of allegiance, is, that a native has a *right*—offered to him by the Constitution—to come under allegiance to the government, if he so please; and thus entitle himself to membership in the body politic. His allegiance cannot be refused. Whereas a foreigner's allegiance can be refused, if the government so please.

IV.

The Constitution certainly supposes that the crime of treason can be committed only by man, as an individual. It would be very curious to see a man indicted, convicted, or hanged, otherwise than as an individual; or accused of having committed his treason otherwise than as an individual. And yet it is clearly impossible that any one can be personally guilty of treason, can be a traitor *in fact,* unless he, as an individual, has in some way voluntarily pledged his faith and fidelity to the government. Certainly no man, or body of men, could pledge it for him, without his consent; and no man, or body of men, have any right to presume it against him, when he has not pledged it himself.

V.

It is plain, therefore, that if, when the Constitution says treason, it means treason—treason in fact, and nothing else—there is no ground at all for pretending that the Southern people have committed that crime. But if, on the other hand, when the Constitution says treason, it means what the Czar and the Kaiser mean by treason, then our government is, in principle, no better than theirs; and has no claim whatever to be considered a free government.

VI.

One essential of a free government is that it rest wholly on voluntary support. And one certain proof that a government is not free, is that it coerces more or less persons to support it, against their will. All governments, the worst on earth, and the most tyrannical on earth, are free governments to that portion of the people who voluntarily support

16

them. And all governments—though the best on earth in other respects—are nevertheless tyrannies to that portion of the people—whether few or many—who are compelled to support them against their will. A government is like a church, or any other institution, in these respects. There is no other criterion whatever, by which to determine whether a government is a free one, or not, than the single one of its depending, or not depending, solely on voluntary support.

VII.

No middle ground is possible on this subject. Either "taxation without consent is robbery," or it is not. If it is *not,* then any number of men, who choose, may at any time associate; call themselves a government; assume absolute authority over all weaker than themselves; plunder them at will; and kill them if they resist. If, on the other hand, "taxation without consent *is* robbery," it necessarily follows that every man who has not consented to be taxed, has the same natural right to defend his property against a tax gatherer, that he has to defend it against a highwayman.

VIII.

It is perhaps unnecessary to say that the principles of this argument are as applicable to the State governments, as to the national one.

The opinions of the South, on the subjects of allegiance and treason, have been equally erroneous with those of the North. The only difference between them, has been, that the South has held that a man was (primarily) under involuntary allegiance to the *State* government; while the North held that he was (primarily) under a similar allegiance to the United States government; whereas, in truth, he was under no involuntary allegiance to either.

IX.

Obviously there can be no law of treason more stringent than has now been stated, consistently with political liberty. In the very nature of things there can never be any liberty for the weaker party, on any other principle; and political liberty always means liberty for the weaker party. It is only the weaker party that is ever oppressed. The strong are always free by virtue of their superior strength. So long as government is a mere contest as to which of two parties shall rule the other, the weaker must always succumb. And whether the contest be carried on with ballots or bullets, the principle is the same; for under the theory of government now prevailing, the ballot either signifies a bullet, or it

17

signifies nothing. And no one can consistently use a ballot, unless he intends to use a bullet, if the latter should be needed to insure submission to the former.

X.

The practical difficulty with our government has been, that most of those who have administered it, have taken it for granted that the Constitution, *as it is written,* was a thing of no importance; that it neither said what it meant, nor meant what it said; that it was gotten up by swindlers, (as many of its authors doubtless were,) who said a great many good things, which they did not mean, and meant a great many bad things, which they dared not say; that these men, under the false pretence of a government resting on the consent of the whole people, designed to entrap them into a government of a part, who should be powerful and fraudulent enough to cheat the weaker portion out of all the good things that were said, but not meant, and subject them to all the bad things that were meant, but not said. And most of those who have administered the government, have assumed that all these swindling intentions were to be carried into effect, in the place of the written Constitution. Of all these swindles, the treason swindle is the most flagitious. It is the most flagitious, because it is equally flagitious, in principle, with any; and it includes all the others. It is the instrumentality by which all the others are made effective. A government that can at pleasure accuse, shoot, and hang men, as traitors, for the one general offence of refusing to surrender themselves and their property unreservedly to its arbitrary will, can practice any and all special and particular oppressions it pleases.

The result—and a natural one—has been that we have had governments, State and national, devoted to nearly every grade and species of crime that governments have ever practised upon their victims; and these crimes have culminated in a war that has cost a million of lives; a war carried on, upon one side, for chattel slavery, and on the other for political slavery; upon neither for liberty, justice, or truth. And these crimes have been committed, and this war waged, by men, and the descendants of men, who, less than a hundred years ago, said that all men were equal, and could owe neither service to individuals, nor allegiance to governments, except with their own consent.

XI.

No attempt or pretence, that was ever carried into practical operation amongst civilized men—unless possibly the pretence of a "Divine Right," on the part of some, to govern and enslave others—embodied so much of shameless absurdity, falsehood, impudence, robbery, usurpation, tyranny, and villany of every kind, as the attempt or pretence of establishing a government *by consent,* and getting the actual consent of only so many as may be necessary to keep the rest in subjection by force. Such a government is a mere conspiracy of the strong against the weak. It no more rests on consent than does the worst government on earth.

What substitute for their consent is offered to the weaker party, whose rights are thus annihilated, struck out of existence, by the stronger? Only this: *Their consent is presumed!* That is, these usurpers condescendingly and graciously *presume* that those whom they enslave, *consent* to surrender their all of life, liberty, and property into the hands of those who thus usurp dominion over them! And it is pretended that this presumption of their consent—when no actual consent has been given—is sufficient to save the rights of the victims, and to justify the usurpers! As well might the highwayman pretend to justify himself by presuming that the traveller *consents* to part with his money. As well might the assassin justify himself by simply *presuming* that his victim consents to part with his life. As well might the holder of chattel slaves attempt to justify himself by presuming that they consent to his authority, and to the whips and the robbery which he practises upon them. The presumption is simply a presumption that the weaker party consent to be slaves.

Such is the presumption on which alone our government relies to justify the power it maintains over its unwilling subjects. And it was to establish that presumption as the inexorable and perpetual law of this country, that so much money and blood have been expended.

No Treason. No. VI.

The Constitution of No Authority.

I.

THE Constitution has no inherent authority or obligation. It has no authority or obligation at all, unless as a contract between man and man. And it does not so much as even purport to be a contract between persons now existing. It purports, at most, to be only a contract between persons living eighty years ago. And it can be supposed to have been a contract then only between persons who had already come to years of discretion, so as to be competent to make reasonable and obligatory contracts. Furthermore, we know, historically, that only a small portion even of the people then existing were consulted on the subject, or asked, or permitted to express either their consent or dissent in any formal manner. Those persons, if any, who did give their consent formally, are all dead now. Most of them have been dead forty, fifty, sixty, or seventy years. *And the Constitution, so far as it was their contract, died with them.* They had no natural power or right to make it obligatory upon their children. It is not only plainly impossible, in the nature of things, that they *could* bind their posterity, but they did not even attempt to bind them. That is to say, the instrument does not purport to be an agreement between any body but "the people" *then* existing; nor does it, either expressly or impliedly, assert any right, power, or disposition, on their part, to bind any body but themselves. Let us see. Its language is:

> "We, the people of the United States [that is, the people *then existing* in the United States], in order to form a more perfect union, insure domestic tranquillity, provide for the common defence, promote the general welfare, and secure the blessings of liberty to ourselves *and our posterity,* do ordain and establish this Constitution for the United States of America."

It is plain, in the first place, that this language, *as an agreement,*

21

purports to be only what it at most really was, viz: a contract between the people *then existing;* and, of necessity, binding, as a contract, only upon those *then existing.* In the second place, the language neither expresses nor implies that they had any intention or desire, nor that they imagined they had any right or power, to *bind* their "posterity" to live under it. It does not say that their "posterity" will, shall, or must live under it. It only says, in effect, that their hopes and motives in adopting it were that it might prove useful to their posterity, as well as to themselves, by promoting their union, safety, tranquillity, liberty, etc.

Suppose an agreement were entered into, in this form:

We, the people of Boston, agree to maintain a fort on Governor's Island, to protect ourselves *and our posterity* against invasion.

This agreement, *as an agreement,* would clearly bind nobody but the people then existing. Secondly, it would assert no right, power, or disposition, on their part, to *compel* their "posterity" to maintain such a fort. It would only indicate that the supposed welfare of their posterity was one of the motives that induced the original parties to enter into the agreement.

When a man says he is building a house for himself *and his posterity,* he does not mean to be understood as saying that he has any thought of *binding* them, nor is it to be inferred that he is so foolish as to imagine that he has any right or power to *bind* them, to live in it. So far as they are concerned, he only means to be understood as saying that his hopes and motives, in building it, are that they, or at least some of them, may find it for their happiness to live in it.

So when a man says he is planting a tree for himself *and his posterity,* he does not mean to be understood as saying that he has any thought of *compelling* them, nor is it to be inferred that he is such a simpleton as to imagine that he has any right or power to compel them, to eat the fruit. So far as they are concerned, he only means to say that his hopes and motives, in planting the tree, are that its fruit may be agreeable to them.

So it was with those who originally adopted the Constitution. Whatever may have been their personal intentions, the legal meaning of their language, so far as their "posterity" was concerned, simply was, that their hopes and motives, in entering into the agreement, were that it might prove useful and acceptable to their posterity; that it might promote their union, safety, tranquillity, and welfare; and that it might tend "to secure to them the blessings of liberty." The language does not assert nor at all imply, any right, power, or disposition, on the part of the original parties to the agreement, to *compel* their "posterity" to live under it. If they had intended to *bind* their posterity to live under it, they should have said that their object was, not "to secure to them the blessings of liberty," but to make slaves of them; for if their "posterity" are bound to live under it, they are nothing less than the slaves of their foolish, tyrannical, and dead grandfathers.

It cannot be said that the Constitution formed "the people of the United States," for all time, into a corporation. It does not speak of "the people" as a corporation, but as individuals. A corporation does not describe itself as "we," nor as "people," nor as "ourselves." Nor does a corporation, in legal language, have any "posterity." It supposes itself to have, and speaks of itself as having, perpetual existence, as a single individuality.

Moreover, no body of men, existing at any one time, have the power to create a perpetual corporation. A corporation can become practically perpetual only by the voluntary accession of new members, as the old ones die off. But for this voluntary accession of new members, the corporation necessarily dies with the death of those who originally composed it.

Legally speaking, therefore, there is, in the Constitution, nothing that professes or attempts to bind the "posterity" of those who establish it.

If, then, those who established the Constitution, had no power to bind, and did not attempt to bind, their posterity, the question arises, whether their posterity have bound themselves? If they have done so, they can have done so in only one or both of these two ways, viz. by voting, and paying taxes.

II.

Let us consider these two matters, voting and tax paying, separately. And first of voting.

All the voting that has ever taken place under the Constitution, has been of such a kind that it not only did not pledge the whole people to support the Constitution, but it did not even pledge any one of them to do so, as the following considerations show.

1. In the very nature of things, the act of voting could bind nobody but

the actual voters. But owing to the property qualifications required, it is probable that, during the first twenty or thirty years under the Constitution, not more than one tenth, fifteenth, or perhaps twentieth of the whole population (black and white, men, women, and minors) were permitted to vote. Consequently, so far as voting was concerned, not more than one tenth, fifteenth, or twentieth of those then existing, could have incurred any obligation to support the Constitution.

At the present time, it is probable that not more than one sixth of the whole population are *permitted* to vote. Consequently, so far as voting is concerned, the other five-sixths can have given no pledge that they will support the Constitution.

2. Of the one-sixth that are *permitted* to vote, probably not more than two-thirds (about one-ninth of the whole population) have *usually* voted. Many never vote at all. Many vote only once in two, three, five, or ten years, in periods of great excitement.

No one, by voting, can be said to pledge himself for any longer period than that for which he votes. If, for example, I vote for an officer who is to hold his office for only a year, I cannot be said to have thereby pledged myself to support the government beyond that term. Therefore, on the ground of actual voting, it probably cannot be said that more than one-ninth, or one-eighth, of the whole population are *usually* under any pledge to support the Constitution.

3. It cannot be said that, by voting, a man pledges himself to support the Constitution, unless the act of voting be a perfectly voluntary one on his part. Yet the act of voting cannot properly be called a voluntary one on the part of any very large number of those who do vote. It is rather a measure of necessity imposed upon them by others, than one of their own choice. On this point I repeat what was said in a former number,[1] viz:

> "In truth, in the case of individuals, their actual voting is not to be taken as proof of consent, *even for the time being.* On the contrary, it is to be considered that, without his consent having even been asked a man finds himself environed by a government that he cannot resist; a government that forces him to pay money, render service, and forego the exercise of many of his natural rights, under peril of weighty punishments. He sees, too, that other men practise this tyranny over him by the use of the ballot. He

[1] See "No Treason, No. 2.

24

sees further, that, if he will but use the ballot himself, he has some chance of relieving himself from this tyranny of others, by subjecting them to his own. In short, he finds himself, without his consent, so situated that, if he use the ballot, he may become a master; if he does not use it, he must become a slave. And he has no other alternative than these two. In self-defence, he attempts the former. His case is analogous to that of a man who has been forced into battle, where he must either kill others, or be killed himself. Because, to save his own life in battle, a man attempts to take the lives of his opponents, it is not to be inferred that the battle is one of his own choosing. Neither in contests with the ballot—which is a mere substitute for a bullet—because, as his only chance of self-preservation, a man uses a ballot, is it to be inferred that the contest is one into which he voluntarily entered; that he voluntarily set up all his own natural rights, as a stake against those of others, to be lost or won by the mere power of numbers. On the contrary, it is to be considered that, in an exigency into which he had been forced by others, and in which no other means of self-defence offered, he, as a matter of necessity, used the only one that was left to him.

"Doubtless the most miserable of men, under the most oppressive government in the world, if allowed the ballot, would use it, if they could see any chance of thereby meliorating their condition. But it would not, therefore, be a legitimate inference that the government itself, that crushes them, was one which they had voluntarily set up, or ever consented to.

"Therefore, a man's voting under the Constitution of the United States, is not to be taken as evidence that he ever freely assented to the Constitution, *even for the time being.* Consequently we have no proof that any very large portion, even of the actual voters of the United States, ever really and voluntarily consented to the Constitution, *even for the time being.* Nor can we ever have such proof, until every man is left perfectly free to consent, or not, without thereby subjecting himself or his property to be disturbed or injured by others."

As we can have no legal knowledge as to who votes from choice, and who from the necessity thus forced upon him, we can have no legal knowledge, *as to any particular individual,* that he voted from choice; or, consequently, that by voting, he consented, or pledged himself, to support the government. Legally speaking, therefore, the act of voting utterly fails to pledge *any one* to support the government. It utterly fails to prove that the government rests upon the voluntary support of any body. On general principles of law and reason, it cannot be said that the government has any voluntary supporters at all, until it can be distinctly shown *who* its voluntary supporters are.

4. As taxation is made compulsory on all, whether they vote or not, a large proportion of those who vote, no doubt do so to prevent their own money being used against themselves; when, in fact, they would have gladly abstained from voting, if they could thereby have saved themselves from taxation alone, to say nothing of being saved from all the other usurpations and tyrannies of the government. To take a man's property without his consent, and then to infer his consent because he attempts, by voting, to prevent that property from being used to his injury, is a very insufficient proof of his consent to support the Constitution. It is, in fact, no proof at all. And as we can have no legal knowledge as to *who* the particular individuals are, if there are any, who are willing to be taxed for the sake of voting, or who would prefer freedom from taxation to the privilege of voting, we can have no legal knowledge that any particular individual consents to be taxed for the sake of voting; or, consequently, consents to support the Constitution.

5. At nearly all elections, votes are given for various candidates for the same office. Those who vote for the unsuccessful candidates cannot properly be said to have voted to sustain the Constitution. They may, with more reason, be supposed to have voted, not to support the Constitution, but specially to prevent the tyranny which they anticipate the successful candidate intends to practise upon them under color of the Constitution; and therefore may reasonably be supposed to have voted against the Constitution itself. This supposition is the more reasonable, inasmuch as such voting is the only mode allowed to them of expressing their dissent to the Constitution.

6. Many votes are usually given for candidates who have no prospect of success. Those who give such votes may reasonably be supposed to have voted as they did, with a special intention, not to support, but to obstruct the execution of, the Constitution; and, therefore, against the Constitution itself.

26

7. As all the different votes are given secretly (by secret ballot), there is no legal means of knowing, from the votes themselves, *who* votes for, and *who* against, the Constitution. Therefore voting affords no legal evidence that *any particular individual* supports the Constitution. And where there can be no legal evidence that *any particular individual* supports the Constitution, it cannot legally be said that anybody supports it. It is clearly impossible to have any legal proof of the intentions of large numbers of men, where there can be no legal proof of the intentions of any particular one of them.

8. There being no legal proof of any man's intentions, in voting, we can only conjecture them. As a conjecture, it is probable that a very large proportion of those who vote, do so on this principle, viz., that if, by voting, they could but get the government into their own hands (or that of their friends), and use its powers against their opponents, they would then willingly support the Constitution; but if their opponents are to have the power, and use it against them, then they would *not* willingly support the Constitution.

In short, men's voluntary support of the Constitution is doubtless, in most cases, wholly contingent upon the question whether, by means of the Constitution, they can make themselves masters, or are to be made slaves.

Such contingent consent as that is, in law and reason, no consent at all.

9. As every body who supports the Constitution by voting (if there are any such) does so secretly (by secret ballot), and in a way to avoid all personal responsibility for the acts of his agents or representatives, it cannot legally or reasonably be said that anybody at all supports the Constitution by voting. No man can reasonably or legally be said to do such a thing as to assent to, or support, the Constitution, *unless he does it openly, and in a way to make himself personally responsible for the acts of his agents, so long as they act within the limits of the power he delegates to them.*

10. As all voting is secret, (by secret ballot,) and as all secret governments are necessarily only secret bands of robbers, tyrants, and murderers, the general fact that our government is practically carried on by means of such voting, only proves that there is among us a secret band of robbers, tyrants and murderers, whose purpose is to rob, enslave, and, so far as necessary to accomplish their purposes, murder, the rest of the people. The simple fact of the existence of such a band does nothing towards proving that "the people of the United States," or

any one of them, voluntarily supports the Constitution.

For all the reasons that have now been given, voting furnishes no legal evidence as to who the particular individuals are (if there are any), who *voluntarily* support the Constitution. It therefore furnishes no legal evidence that any body supports it *voluntarily.*

So far, therefore, as voting is concerned, the Constitution, legally speaking, has no supporters at all.

And, as matter of fact, there is not the slightest probability that the Constitution has a single *bona fide* supporter in the country. That is to say, there is not the slightest probability that there is a single man in the country, who both understands what the Constitution really is, *and sincerely supports it for what it really is.*

The ostensible supporters of the Constitution, like the ostensible supporters of most other governments, are made up of three classes, viz.: 1. Knaves, a numerous and active class, who see in the government an instrument which they can use for their own aggrandizement or wealth. 2. Dupes—a large class, no doubt—each of whom, because he is allowed one voice out of millions in deciding what he may do with his own person and his own property, and because he is permitted to have the same voice in robbing, enslaving, and murdering others, that others have in robbing, enslaving, and murdering himself, is stupid enough to imagine that he is a "free man," a "sovereign"; that this is "a free government"; "a government of equal rights," "the best government on earth,"[2] and such like absurdities. 3. A class who have some appreciation of the evils of government, but either do not see how to get rid of them, or do not choose to so far sacrifice their private interests as to give themselves seriously and earnestly to the work of making a change.

III.

The payment of taxes, being compulsory, of course furnishes no evidence that any one voluntarily supports the Constitution.

It is true that the *theory* of our Constitution is, that all taxes are paid voluntarily; that our government is a mutual insurance company, voluntarily entered into by the people with each other; that each man makes a free and purely voluntary contract with all others who are parties to the Constitution, to pay so much money for so much

[2]Suppose it be "the best government on earth," does that prove its own goodness, or only the badness of all other governments?

protection, the same as he does with any other insurance company; and that he is just as free not to be protected, and not to pay any tax, as he is to pay a tax, and be protected.

But this theory of our government is wholly different from the practical fact. The fact is that the government, like a highwayman, says to a man: *Your money, or your life.* And many, if not most, taxes are paid under the compulsion of that threat.

The government does not, indeed, waylay a man in a lonely place, spring upon him from the road side, and, holding a pistol to his head, proceed to rifle his pockets. But the robbery is none the less a robbery on that account; and it is far more dastardly and shameful.

The highwayman takes solely upon himself the responsibility, danger, and crime of his own act. He does not pretend that he has any rightful claim to your money, or that he intends to use it for your own benefit. He does not pretend to be anything but a robber. He has not acquired impudence enough to profess to be merely a "protector," and that he takes men's money against their will, merely to enable him to "protect" those infatuated travellers, who feel perfectly able to protect themselves, or do not appreciate his peculiar system of protection. He is too sensible a man to make such professions as these. Furthermore, having taken your money, he leaves you, as you wish him to do. He does not persist in following you on the road, against your will; assuming to be your rightful "sovereign," on account of the "protection" he affords you. He does not keep "protecting" you, by commanding you to bow down and serve him; by requiring you to do this, and forbidding you to do that; by robbing you of more money as often as he finds it for his interest or pleasure to do so; and by branding you as a rebel, a traitor, and an enemy to your country, and shooting you down without mercy, if you dispute his authority, or resist his demands. He is too much of a gentleman to be guilty of such impostures, and insults, and villanies as these. In short, he does not, in addition to robbing you, attempt to make you either his dupe or his slave.

The proceedings of those robbers and murderers, who call themselves "the government," are directly the opposite of these of the single highwayman.

In the first place, they do not, like him, make themselves individually known; or, consequently, take upon themselves personally the responsibility of their acts. On the contrary, they secretly (by secret ballot) designate some one of their number to commit the robbery in their behalf, while they keep themselves practically concealed. They say to the person thus designated:

Go to A— B—, and say to him that "the government" has need of money to meet the expenses of protecting him and his property. If he presumes to say that he has never contracted with us to protect him, and that he wants none of our protection, say to him that that is our business, and not his; that we *choose* to protect him, whether he desires us to do so or not; and that we demand pay, too, for protecting him. If he dares to inquire who the individuals are, who have thus taken upon themselves the title of "the government," and who assume to protect him, and demand payment of him, without his having ever made any contract with them, say to him that that, too, is our business, and not his; that we do not *choose* to make ourselves *individually* known to him; that we have secretly (by secret ballot) appointed you our agent to give him notice of our demands, and, if he complies with them, to give him, in our name, a receipt that will protect him against any similar demand *for the present year*. If he refuses to comply, seize and sell enough of his property to pay not only our demands, but all your own expenses and trouble beside. If he resists the seizure of his property, call upon the bystanders to help you (doubtless some of them will prove to be members of our band). If, in defending his property, he should kill any of our band who are assisting you, capture him at all hazards; charge him (in one of our courts) with murder, convict him, and hang him. If he should call upon his neighbors, or any others who, like him, may be disposed to resist our demands, and they should come in large numbers to his assistance, cry out that they are all rebels and traitors; that "our country" is in danger; call upon the commander of our hired murderers; tell him to quell the rebellion and "save the country," cost what it may. Tell him to kill all who resist, though they should be hundreds of thousands; and thus strike terror into all others similarly disposed. See that the work of murder is thoroughly done, that we may have no further trouble of this kind hereafter. When these traitors shall have thus been taught our strength and our determination, they will be good loyal citizens for many years, and pay their taxes without a why or a wherefore.

It is under such compulsion as this that taxes, so called, are paid. And how much proof the payment of taxes affords, that the people *consent* to support "the government," it needs no further argument to show.

2. Still another reason why the payment of taxes implies no consent, or pledge, to support the government, is that the tax payer does not know,

30

and has no means of knowing, who the particular individuals are who compose "the government." To him "the government" is a myth, an abstraction, an incorporeality, with which he can make no contract, and to which he can give no consent, and make no pledge. He knows it only through its pretended agents. "The government" itself he never sees. He knows indeed, by common report, that certain persons, of a certain age, are *permitted* to vote; and thus to *make* themselves parts of, or (if they choose) opponents of, the government, for the time being. But who of them do thus vote, and especially *how* each one votes (whether so as to aid or oppose the government), he does not know; the voting being all done secretly (by secret ballot). Who, therefore, practically compose "the government," for the time being, he has no means of knowing. Of course he can make no contract with them, give them no consent, and make them no pledge. Of necessity, therefore, his paying taxes to them implies, on his part, no contract, consent, or pledge to support them—that is, to support "the government," or the Constitution.

3. Not knowing who the particular individuals are, who call themselves "the government," the tax payer does not know whom he pays his taxes to. All he knows is that a man comes to him, representing himself to be the agent of "the government"—that is, the agent of a secret band of robbers and murderers, who have taken to themselves the title of "the government," and have determined to kill every body who refuses to give them whatever money they demand. To save his life, he gives up his money to this agent. But as this agent does not make his principals individually known to the tax payer, the latter, after he has given up his money, knows no more who are "the government"—that is, who were the robbers—than he did before. To say, therefore, that by giving up his money to their agent, he entered into a voluntary contract with them, that he pledges himself to obey them, to support them, and to give them whatever money they should demand of him in the future, is simply ridiculous.

4. All political power, as it is called, rests practically upon this matter of money. Any number of scoundrels, having money enough to start with, can establish themselves as a "government;" because, with money, they can hire soldiers, and with soldiers extort more money; and also compel general obedience to their will. It is with government, as Cæsar said it was in war, that money and soldiers mutually supported each other; that with money he could hire soldiers, and with soldiers extort money. So these villains, who call themselves governments, well understand that their power rests primarily upon money. With money they can

31

hire soldiers, and with soldiers extort money. And, when their authority is denied, the first use they always make of money, is to hire soldiers to kill or subdue all who refuse them more money.

For this reason, whoever desires liberty, should understand these vital facts, viz.: 1. That every man who puts money into the hands of a "government" (so called), puts into its hands a sword which will be used against himself, to extort more money from him, and also to keep him in subjection to its arbitrary will. 2. That those who will take his money, without his consent, in the first place, will use it for his further robbery and enslavement, if he presumes to resist their demands in the future. 3. That it is a perfect absurdity to suppose that any body of men would ever take a man's money without his consent, for any such object as they profess to take it for, viz., that of protecting him; for why should they wish to protect him, if he does not wish them to do so? To suppose that they would do so, is just as absurd as it would be to suppose that they would take his money without his consent, for the purpose of buying food or clothing for him, when he did not want it. 4. If a man wants "protection," he is competent to make his own bargains for it; and nobody has any occasion to rob him, in order to "protect" him against his will. 5. That the only security men can have for their political liberty, consists in their keeping their money in their own pockets, until they have assurances, perfectly satisfactory to themselves, that it will be used as they wish it to be used, for their benefit, and not for their injury. 6. That no government, so called, can reasonably be trusted for a moment, or reasonably be supposed to have honest purposes in view, any longer than it depends wholly upon voluntary support.

These facts are all so vital and so self-evident, that it cannot reasonably be supposed that any one will *voluntarily* pay money to a "government," for the purpose of securing its protection, unless he first makes an explicit and purely voluntary contract with it for that purpose.

It is perfectly evident, therefore, that neither such voting, nor such payment of taxes, as actually takes place, proves anybody's consent, or obligation, to support the Constitution. Consequently we have no evidence at all that the Constitution is binding upon anybody, or that anybody is under any contract or obligation whatever to support it. And nobody *is* under any obligation to support it.

The Constitution not only binds nobody now, but it never did bind anybody. It never bound anybody, because it was never agreed to by any body in such a manner as to make it, on general principles of law and reason, binding upon him.

It is a general principle of law and reason, that a *written* instrument binds no one until he has signed it. This principle is so inflexible a one, that even though a man is unable to write his name, he must still "make his mark," before he is bound by a written contract. This custom was established ages ago, when few men could write their names; when a clerk—that is, a man who could write—was so rare and valuable a person, that even if he were guilty of high crimes, he was entitled to pardon, on the ground that the public could not afford to lose his services. Even at that time, a written contract must be signed; and men who could not write, either "made their mark," or signed their contracts by stamping their seals upon wax affixed to the parchment on which their contracts were written. Hence the custom of affixing seals, that has continued to this time.

The law holds, and reason declares, that if a written instrument is not signed, the presumption must be that the party to be bound by it, did not choose to sign it, or to bind himself by it. And law and reason both give him until the last moment, in which to decide whether he will sign it, or not. Neither law nor reason requires or expects a man to agree to an instrument, *until it is written;* for until it is written, he cannot know its precise legal meaning. And when it is written, and he has had the opportunity to satisfy himself of its precise legal meaning, he is then expected to decide, and not before, whether he will agree to it or not. And if he do not *then* sign it, his reason is supposed to be, that he does not choose to enter into such a contract. The fact that the instrument was written *for him to sign,* or with the hope that he would sign it, goes for nothing.

Where would be the end of fraud and litigation, if one party could bring into court a written instrument, *without any signature,* and claim to have it enforced, upon the ground that it was written for another man to sign? that this other man had promised to sign it? that he ought to have signed it? that he had had the opportunity to sign it, if he would? but that he had refused or neglected to do so? yet that is the most that could ever be said of the Constitution.[3] The very judges, who

[3]The very men who drafted it, never signed it in any way to bind themselves by it, *as a contract.* And not one of them probably ever would have signed it in any way to bind himself by it, *as a contract.*

profess to derive all their authority from the Constitution—from an instrument that nobody ever signed—would spurn any other instrument, not signed, that should be brought before them for adjudication.

Moreover, a written instrument must, in law and reason, not only be signed, but must also be delivered to the party (or to some one for him), in whose favor it is made, before it can bind the party making it. The signing is of no effect, unless the instrument be also delivered. And a party is at perfect liberty to refuse to deliver a written instrument, after he has signed it. He is as free to refuse to deliver it, as he is to refuse to sign it. The constitution was not only never signed by anybody, but it was never delivered by anybody to anybody, or to anybody's agent or attorney. It can therefore be of no more validity as a contract, than can any other instrument, that was never signed or delivered.

V

As further evidence of the general sense of mankind, as to the practical necessity there is that all men's *important* contracts, especially those of a permanent nature, should be both written and signed, the following facts are pertinent.

For nearly two hundred years—that is, since 1677—there has been on the statute book of England, and the same, in substance, if not precisely in letter, has been re-enacted, and is now in force, in nearly or quite all the States of this Union, a statute, the general object of which is to declare that no action shall be brought to enforce contracts of the more important class, *unless they are put in writing, and signed by the parties to be held chargeable upon them.*[4]

[4]I have personally examined the statute books of the following States, viz.: Maine, New Hampshire, Vermont, Massachusetts, Rhode Island, Connecticut, New York, New Jersey, Pennsylvania, Delaware, Virginia, North Carolina, South Carolina, Georgia, Florida, Alabama, Mississippi, Tennessee, Kentucky, Ohio, Michigan, Indiana, Illinois, Wisconsin, Texas, Arkansas, Missouri, Iowa, Minnesota, Nebraska, Kansas, Nevada, California, and Oregon, and find that in all these States the English statute has been re-enacted, sometimes with modifications, but generally enlarging its operations, and is now in force.

The following are some of the provisions of the Massachusetts statute:

"No action shall be brought in any of the following cases, that is to say: . . . .

"To charge a person upon a special promise to answer for the debt, default, or misdoings of another: . . . .

"Upon a contract for the sale of lands, tenements, hereditaments, or of any interest in, or concerning them; or

"Upon an agreement that is not to be performed within one year from the writing thereof:

"Unless the promise, contract, or agreement, upon which such action is brought, or some memorandum or note thereof, is in writing, and signed by the party to be charged therewith, or by some person thereunto by

34

The principle of the statute, be it observed, is, not merely that written contracts shall be signed, but also that all contracts, except those specially exempted—generally those that are for small amounts, and are to remain in force but for a short time—*shall be both written and signed.*

The reason of the statute, on this point, is, that it is now so easy a thing for men to put their contracts in writing, and sign them, and their failure to do so opens the door to so much doubt, fraud, and litigation, that men who neglect to have their contracts—of any considerable importance—written and signed, ought not to have the benefit of courts of justice to enforce them. And this reason is a wise one; and that experience has confirmed its wisdom and necessity, is demonstrated by the fact that it has been acted upon in England for nearly two hundred years, and has been so nearly universally adopted in this country, and that nobody thinks of repealing it.

We all know, too, how careful most men are to have their contracts written and signed, even when this statute does not require it. For example, most men, if they have money due them, of no larger amount than five or ten dollars, are careful to take a note for it. If they buy even a small bill of goods, paying for it at the time of delivery, they take a receipted bill for it. If they pay a small balance of a book account, or any other small debt previously contracted, they take a written receipt for it.

Furthermore, the law everywhere (probably) in our country, as well as in England, requires that a large class of contracts, such as wills, deeds, etc., shall not only be written and signed, but also sealed, witnessed, and acknowledged. And in the case of married women conveying their rights in real estate, the law, in many States, requires that the women shall be examined separate and apart from their husbands, and declare that they sign their contracts free of any fear or compulsion of their husbands.

Such are some of the precautions which the laws require, and which individuals—from motives of common prudence, even in cases not required by law—take, to put their contracts in writing, and have them signed, &c., to guard against all uncertainties and controversies in

him awfully authorized: . . . .

"No contract for the sale of goods, wares, or merchandise, for the price of fifty dollars or more, shall be good or valid, unless the purchaser accepts and receives part of the goods so sold, or gives something in earnest to bind the bargain, or in part payment; or unless some note or memorandum in writing of the bargain is made and signed by the party to be charged thereby, or by some person thereunto by him lawfully authorized."

regard to their meaning and validity. And yet we have what purports, or professes, or is claimed, to be a contract—the Constitution—made eighty years ago, by men who are now all dead, and who never had any power to bind *us,* but which (it is claimed) has nevertheless bound three generations of men, consisting of many millions, and which (it is claimed) will be binding upon all the millions that are to come; but which nobody ever signed, sealed, delivered, witnessed, or acknowledged; and which few persons, compared with the whole number that are claimed to be bound by it, have ever read, or even seen, or ever will read, or see. And of those who ever have read it, or ever will read it, scarcely any two, perhaps no two, have ever agreed, or ever will agree, as to what it means.

Moreover, this supposed contract, which would not be received in any court of justice sitting under its authority, if offered to prove a debt of five dollars, owing by one man to another, is one by which—*as it is generally interpreted by those who pretend to administer it*—all men, women and children throughout the country, and through all time, surrender not only all their property, but also their liberties, and even lives, into the hands of men who by this supposed contract, are expressly made wholly irresponsible for their disposal of them. And we are so insane, or so wicked, as to destroy property and lives without limit, in fighting to compel men to fulfil a supposed contract, which, inasmuch as it has never been signed by anybody, is, on general principles of law and reason—such principles as we are all governed by in regard to other contracts—the merest waste paper, binding upon nobody, fit only to be thrown into the fire; or, if preserved, preserved only to serve as a witness and a warning of the folly and wickedness of mankind.

VI.

It is no exaggeration, but a literal truth, to say that, by the Constitution —*not as I interpret it, but as it is interpreted by those who pretend to administer it*—the properties, liberties, and lives of the entire people of the United States are surrendered unreservedly into the hands of men who, it is provided by the Constitution itself, shall never be "questioned" as to any disposal they make of them.

Thus the Constitution (Art. 1, Sec. 6) provides that, "for any speech or debate or vote, in either house, they the senators and representatives shall not be questioned in any other place."

The whole law-making power is given to these senators and

representatives, when acting by a two-thirds vote[5]; and this provision protects them from all responsibility for the laws they make.

The Constitution also enables them to secure the execution of all their laws, by giving them power to withhold the salaries of, and to impeach and remove, all judicial and executive officers, who refuse to execute them.

Thus the whole power of the government is in their hands, and they are made utterly irresponsible for the use they make of it. What is this but absolute, irresponsible power?

It is no answer to this view of the case to say that these men are under oath to use their power only within certain limits; for what care they, or what should they care, for oaths or limits, when it is expressly provided, by the Constitution itself, that they shall never be "questioned," or held to any responsibility whatever, for violating their oaths, or transgressing those limits?

Neither is it any answer to this view of the case to say that the particular individuals holding this power can be changed once in two or six years; for the power of each set of men is absolute during the term for which they hold it; and when they can hold it no longer, they are succeeded only by men whose power will be equally absolute and irresponsible.

Neither is it any answer to this view of the case to say that the men holding this absolute, irresponsible power, must be men chosen by the people (or portions of them) to hold it. A man is none the less a slave because he is allowed to choose a new master once in a term of years. Neither are a people any the less slaves because permitted periodically to choose new masters. What makes them slaves is the fact that they now are, and are always hereafter to be, in the hands of men whose power over them is, and always is to be, absolute and irresponsible.[6]

The right of absolute and irresponsible dominion is the right of property, and the right of property is the right of absolute, irresponsible dominion. The two are identical; the one necessarily implying the other. Neither can exist without the other. If, therefore, Congress have that absolute and irresponsible law-making power, which the Constitution—according to their interpretation of it—gives them, it

---

[5] And this two-thirds vote may be but two-thirds of a quorum—that is two-thirds of a majority—instead of two-thirds of the whole.

[6] Of what appreciable value is it to any man, as an individual, that he is allowed a voice in choosing these public masters? His voice is only one of several millions.

can only be because they own us as property. If they own us as property, they are our masters, and their will is our law. If they do not own us as property, they are not our masters, and their will, *as such,* is of no authority over us.

But these men who claim and exercise this absolute and irresponsible dominion over us, dare not be consistent, and claim either to be our masters, or to own us as property. They say they are only our servants, agents, attorneys, and representatives. But this declaration involves an absurdity, a contradiction. No man can be my servant, agent, attorney, or representative, and be, at the same time, uncontrollable by me, and irresponsible to me for his acts. It is of no importance that I appointed him, and put all power in his hands. If I made him uncontrollable by me, and irresponsible to me, he is no longer my servant, agent, attorney, or representative. If I gave him absolute, irresponsible power over my property, I gave him the property. If I gave him absolute, irresponsible power over myself, I made him my master, and gave myself to him as a slave. And it is of no importance whether I *called him* master or servant, agent or owner. The only question is, what power did I put into his hands? Was it an absolute and irresponsible one? or a limited and responsible one?

For still another reason they are neither our servants, agents, attorneys, nor representatives. And that reason is, that we do not make ourselves responsible for their acts. If a man is my servant, agent, or attorney, I necessarily make myself responsible for all his acts done within the limits of the power I have intrusted to him. If I have intrusted him, as my agent, with either absolute power, or any power at all, over the persons or properties of other men than myself, I thereby necessarily make myself responsible to those other persons for any injuries he may do them, so long as he acts within the limits of the power I have granted him. But no individual who may be injured in his person or property, by acts of Congress, can come to the individual electors, and hold them responsible for these acts of their so-called agents or representatives. This fact proves that these pretended agents of the people, of everybody, are really the agents of nobody.

If, then, nobody is individually responsible for the acts of Congress, the members of Congress are nobody's agents. And if they are nobody's agents, they are themselves individually responsible for their own acts, and for the acts of all whom they employ. And the authority they are exercising is simply their own individual authority; and, by the law of nature—the highest of all laws—anybody injured by their acts, anybody who is deprived by them of his property or his liberty, has the same right to hold them individually responsible, that he has to hold any other trespasser individually responsible. He has the same right to resist them, and their agents, that he has to resist any other trespassers.

VII.

It is plain, then, that on general principles of law and reason—such principles as we all act upon in courts of justice and in common life— the Constitution is no contract; that it binds nobody, and never did bind anybody; and that all those who pretend to act by its authority, are really acting without any legitimate authority at all; that, on general principles of law and reason, they are mere usurpers, and that everybody not only has the right, but is morally bound, to treat them as such.

If the people of this country wish to maintain such a government as the Constitution describes, there is no reason in the world why they should not sign the instrument itself, and thus make known their wishes in an open, authentic manner; in such manner as the common sense and experience of mankind have shown to be reasonable and necessary in such cases; *and in such manner as to make themselves (as they ought to do) individually responsible for the acts of the government.* But the people have never been asked to sign it. And the only reason why they have never been asked to sign it, has been that it has been known that they never would sign it; that they were neither such fools nor knaves as they must needs have been to be willing to sign it; that (at least as it has been practically interpreted) it is not what any sensible and honest man wants for himself; nor such as he has any right to impose upon others. It is, to all moral intents and purposes, as destitute of obligation as the compacts which robbers and thieves and pirates enter into with each other, but never sign.

If any considerable number of the people believe the Constitution to be good, why do they not sign it themselves, and make laws for, and administer them upon, each other; leaving all other persons (who do not interfere with them) in peace? Until they have tried the experiment for themselves, how can they have the face to impose the Constitution upon, or even to recommend it to, others? Plainly the reason for such absurd and inconsistent conduct is that they want the Constitution, not solely for any honest or legitimate use it can be of to themselves or others, but for the dishonest and illegitimate power it gives them over the persons and properties of others. But for this latter reason, all their eulogiums on the Constitution, all their exhortations, and all their

39

expenditures of money and blood to sustain it, would be wanting.

VIII.

The Constitution itself, then, being of no authority, on what authority does our government practically rest? On what ground can those who pretend to administer it, claim the right to seize men's property, to restrain them of their natural liberty of action, industry, and trade, and to kill all who deny their authority to dispose of men's properties, liberties, and lives at their pleasure or discretion?

The most they can say, in answer to this question, is, that some half, two-thirds, or three-fourths of the male adults of the country have a *tacit understanding* that they will maintain a government under the Constitution; that they will select, by ballot, the persons to administer it; and that those persons who may receive a majority, or a plurality, of their ballots, shall act as their representatives, and administer the Constitution in their name, and by their authority.

But this tacit understanding (admitting it to exist) cannot at all justify the conclusion drawn from it. A tacit understanding between A, B, and C, that they will, by ballot, depute D as their agent, to deprive me of my property, liberty, or life, cannot at all authorize D to do so. He is none the less a robber, tyrant, and murderer, because he claims to act as their agent, than he would be if he avowedly acted on his own responsibility alone.

Neither am I bound to recognize him as their agent, nor can he legitimately claim to be their agent, when he brings no *written* authority from them accrediting him as such. I am under no obligation to take his word as to who his principals may be, or whether he has any. Bringing no credentials, I have a right to say he has no such authority even as he claims to have: and that he is therefore intending to rob, enslave, or murder me on his own account.

This tacit understanding, therefore, among the voters of the country, amounts to nothing as an authority to their agents. Neither do the ballots by which they select their agents, avail any more than does their tacit understanding; for their ballots are given in secret, and therefore in a way to avoid any personal responsibility for the acts of their agents.

No body of men can be said to authorize a man to act as their agent, to the injury of a third person, unless they do it in so open and authentic a manner as to make themselves personally responsible for his acts. None of the voters in this country appoint their political agents in any open

40

authentic manner, or in any manner to make themselves responsible for their acts. Therefore these pretended agents cannot legitimately claim to be really agents. Somebody must be responsible for the acts of these pretended agents; and if they cannot show any open and authentic credentials from their principals, they cannot, in law or reason, be said to have any principals. The maxim applies here, that what does not appear, does not exist. If they can show no principals, they have none.

But even these pretended agents do not themselves know who their pretended principals are. These latter act in secret; for acting by secret ballot is acting in secret as much as if they were to meet in secret conclave in the darkness of the night. And they are personally as much unknown to the agents they select, as they are to others. No pretended agent therefore can ever know by whose ballots he is selected, or consequently who his real principals are. Not knowing who his principals are, he has no right to say that he has any. He can, at most, say only that he is the agent of a secret band of robbers and murderers, who are bound by that faith which prevails among confederates in crime, to stand by him, if his acts, done in their name, shall be resisted.

Men honestly engaged in attempting to establish justice in the world, have no occasion thus to act in secret; or to appoint agents to do acts for which they (the principals) are not willing to be responsible.

The secret ballot makes a secret government; and a secret government is a secret band of robbers and murderers. Open despotism is better than this. The single despot stands out in the face of all men, and says: I am the State: My will is law: I am your master: I take the responsibility of my acts: The only arbiter I acknowledge is the sword: If any one denies my right, let him try conclusions with me.

But a secret government is little less than a government of assassins. Under it, a man knows not who his tyrants are, until they have struck, and perhaps not then. He may *guess,* beforehand, as to some of his immediate neighbors. But he really *knows* nothing. The man to whom he would most naturally fly for protection, may prove an enemy, when the time of trial comes.

This is the kind of government we have; and it is the only one we are likely to have, until men are ready to say: We will consent to no Constitution, except such an one as we are neither ashamed nor afraid to sign; and we will authorize no government to do any thing in our name which we are not willing to be personally responsible for.

IX.

What is the motive to the secret ballot? This, and only this: Like other confederates in crime, those who use it are not friends, but enemies; and they are afraid to be known, and to have their individual doings known, even to each other. They can contrive to bring about a sufficient understanding to enable them to act in concert against other persons; but beyond this they have no confidence, and no friendship, among themselves. In fact, they are engaged quite as much in schemes for plundering each other, as in plundering those who are not of them. And it is perfectly well understood among them that the strongest party among them will, in certain contingencies, murder each other by the hundreds of thousands (as they lately did do) to accomplish their purposes against each other. Hence they dare not be known, and have their individual doings known, even to each other. And this is avowedly the only reason for the ballot: for a secret government; a government by secret bands of robbers and murderers. And we are insane enough to call this liberty! To be a member of this secret band of robbers and murderers is esteemed a privilege and an honor! Without this privilege, a man is considered a slave; but with it a free man! With it he is considered a free man, because he has the same power to secretly (by secret ballot) procure the robbery, enslavement, and murder of another man, that that other man has to procure his robbery, enslavement, and murder. And this they call equal rights!

If any number of men, many or few, claim the right to govern the people of this country, let them make and sign an open compact with each other to do so. Let them thus make themselves individually known to those whom they propose to govern. And let them thus openly take the legitimate responsibility of their acts. How many of those who now support the Constitution, will ever do this? How many will ever dare openly proclaim their right to govern? or take the legitimate responsibility of their acts? Not one!

X.

It is obvious that, on general principles of law and reason, there exists no such thing as a government created by, or resting upon, any consent, compact, or agreement of "the people of the United States" with each other; that the only visible, tangible, responsible government that exists, is that of a few individuals only, who act in concert, and call themselves by the several names of senators, representatives, presidents, judges, marshals, treasurers, collectors, generals, colonels, captains, &c., &c.

On general principles of law and reason, it is of no importance whatever that these few individuals *profess* to be the agents and representatives of "the people of the United States"; since they can show no credentials from the people themselves; they were never appointed as agents or representatives in any open authentic manner; they do not themselves know, and have no means of knowing, and cannot prove, who their principals (as they call them) are individually; and consequently cannot, in law or reason, be said to have any principals at all.

It is obvious, too, that if these alleged principals ever did appoint these pretended agents, or representatives, they appointed them secretly (by secret ballot), and in a way to avoid all personal responsibility for their acts; that, at most, these alleged principals put these pretended agents forward for the most criminal purposes, viz.: to plunder the people of their property, and restrain them of their liberty; and that the only authority that these alleged principals have for so doing, is simply a *tacit understanding* among themselves that they will imprison, shoot, or hang every man who resists the exactions and restraints which their agents or representatives may impose upon them.

Thus it is obvious that the only visible, tangible government we have is made up of these professed agents or representatives of a secret band of robbers and murderers, who, to cover up, or gloss over, their robberies and murders, have taken to themselves the title of "the people of the United States;" and who, on the pretence of being "the people of the United States," assert their right to subject to their dominion, and to control and dispose of at their pleasure, all property and persons found in the United States.

XI.

On general principles of law and reason, the oaths which these pretended agents of the people take "to support the Constitution," are of no validity or obligation. And why? For this, if for no other reason, viz. *that they are given to nobody.* There is no privity, (as the lawyers say),—that is, no mutual recognition, consent and agreement— between those who take these oaths, and any other persons.

If I go upon Boston Common, and in the presence of a hundred thousand people, men, women and children, with whom I have no contract on the subject, take an oath that I will enforce upon them the laws of Moses, of Lycurgus, of Solon, of Justinian, or of Alfred, that oath is, on general principles of law and reason, of no obligation. It is of no obligation, not merely because it is intrinsically a criminal one, *but also because it is given to nobody,* and consequently pledges my faith to nobody. It is merely given to the winds.

It would not alter the case at all to say that, among these hundred thousand persons, in whose presence the oath was taken, there were two, three, or five thousand male adults, who had *secretly*—by secret ballot, and in a way to avoid making themselves *individually* known to me, or to the remainder of the hundred thousand—designated me as their agent to rule, control, plunder, and, if need be, murder, these hundred thousand people. The fact that they had designated me *secretly,* and in a manner to prevent my knowing them *individually,* prevents all *privity* between them and me; and consequently makes it impossible that there can be any contract, or pledge of faith, on my part towards them; for it is impossible that I can pledge my faith, in any legal sense, to a man whom I neither know, nor have any means of knowing, *individually.*

So far as I am concerned, then, these two, three, or five thousand persons are a secret band of robbers and murderers, who have secretly, and in a way to save themselves from all responsibility for my acts, designated me as their agent; and have, through some other agent, or pretended agent, made their wishes known to me. But being, nevertheless, individually unknown to me, and having no open, authentic contract with me, my oath is, on general principles of law and reason, of no validity as a pledge of faith *to them.* And being no pledge of faith *to them,* it is no pledge of faith to anybody. It is mere idle wind. At most, it is only a pledge of faith to an unknown band of robbers and murderers, whose instrument for plundering and murdering other people, I thus publicly confess myself to be. And it has no other obligation than a similar oath given to any other unknown body of pirates, robbers, and murderers.

For these reasons the oath taken by members of Congress, "to support the Constitution," are, on general principles of law and reason, of no validity. They are not only criminal in themselves, and therefore void; but they are also void for the further reason *that they are given to nobody.*

It cannot be said that, in any legitimate or legal sense, they are given to "the people of the United States;" because neither the whole, nor any large proportion of the whole, people of the United States ever, either openly or secretly, appointed or designated these men as their agents to carry the Constitution into effect. The great body of the people—that is, men, women and children—were never asked, or even permitted, to signify, in any *formal* manner, either openly or secretly, their choice or wish on the subject. The most that these members of Congress can say, in favor of their appointment, is simply this: Each one can say for himself:

I have evidence satisfactory to myself, that there exists, scattered throughout the country, a band of men, having a tacit understanding with each other, and calling themselves "the people of the United States," whose general purposes are to control and plunder each other, and all other persons in the country, and, so far as they can, even in neighboring countries; and to kill every man who shall attempt to defend his person and property against their schemes of plunder and dominion. Who these men are, *individually,* I have no certain means of knowing, for they sign no papers, and give no open, authentic evidence of their *individual* membership. They are not known individually even to each other. They are apparently as much afraid of being individually known to each other, as of being known to other persons. Hence they *ordinarily* have no mode either of exercising, or of making known, their individual membership, otherwise than by giving their votes *secretly* for certain agents to do their will. But although these men are individually unknown, both to each other and to other persons, it is generally understood in the country that none but male persons, of the age of twenty-one years and upwards, can be members. It is also generally understood that *all* male persons, born in the country, having certain complexions, and (in some localities) certain amounts of property, and (in certain cases) even persons of foreign birth, are *permitted* to be members. But it appears that usually not more than one-half, two-thirds, or, in some cases, three-fourths, of all who are thus *permitted* to become members of the band, ever exercise, or consequently prove, their actual membership, in the only mode in which they ordinarily can exercise or prove it, viz., by giving their votes *secretly* for the officers or agents of the band. The number of these secret votes, so far as we have any account of them, varies greatly from year to year, thus tending to prove that the band, instead of being a permanent organization, is a merely *pro tempore* affair with those who choose to act with it for the time being. The gross number of these secret votes, or what purports to be their gross number, in different localities, is occasionally published. Whether these reports are accurate or not, we have no means of knowing. It is generally supposed that great frauds are often committed in depositing them. They are understood to be received and counted by certain men, who are themselves appointed for that purpose by the same secret process by which all other officers and agents of the band are selected. According to the reports of these receivers of votes (for whose accuracy or honesty, however, I cannot vouch), and according to my best knowledge of the whole number of male persons "in my district," who (it is supposed) were *permitted* to vote, it would appear that one-half, two-thirds or three-fourths actually did vote. Who the men were, *individually,* who cast these votes, I have no knowledge, for the whole thing was done secretly. But of the secret votes thus given for what they call a "member of Congress," the receivers reported that I had a majority, or at least a larger number than any other one person. And it is only by virtue of such a designation that I am now here to act in concert with other persons similarly selected in other parts of the country. It is understood among those who sent me here, that all the persons so selected, will, on coming together at the City of Washington, take an oath in each other's presence "to support the Constitution of the United States." By this is meant a certain paper that was drawn up eighty years ago. It was never signed by anybody, and apparently has no obligation, and never had any obligation, as a contract. In fact, few persons ever read it, and doubtless much the largest number of those who voted for me and the others, never even saw it, or now pretend to know what it means. Nevertheless, it is often spoken of in the country as "the Constitution of the United States;" and for some reason or another, the men who sent me here, seem to expect that I, and all with whom I act, will swear to carry this Constitution into effect. I am therefore ready to take this oath, and to co-operate with all others, similarly selected, who are ready to take the same oath.

This is the most that any member of Congress can say in proof that he has any constituency; that he represents anybody; that his oath "to support the Constitution," *is given to anybody,* or pledges his faith *to anybody.* He has no open, written, or other authentic evidence, such as is required in all other cases, that he was ever appointed the agent or representative of anybody. He has no written power of attorney from any single individual. He has no such legal knowledge as is required in all other cases, by which he can identify a single one of those who pretend to have appointed him to represent them.

Of course his oath, professedly given to them, "to support the Constitution," is, on general principles of law and reason, an oath given to nobody. It pledges his faith to nobody. If he fails to fulfil his oath, not a single person can come forward, and say to him, you have betrayed *me,* or broken faith with *me.*

No one can come forward and say to him: I appointed you *my* attorney to act for *me.* I required you to swear that, as *my* attorney, you would support the Constitution. You promised *me* that you would do so; and now you have forfeited the oath you gave to *me.* No single individual can say this.

No open, avowed, or responsible association, or body of men, can come forward and say to him: *We* appointed you *our* attorney, to act for *us. We* required you to swear that, as *our* attorney, you would support the Constitution. You promised *us* that you would do so; and now you have forfeited the oath you gave to *us.*

No open, avowed, or responsible association, or body of men, can say this to him; because there is no such association or body of men in existence. If any one should assert that there is such an association, let him prove, if he can, who compose it. Let him produce, if he can, any open, written, or other authentic contract, signed or agreed to by these men; forming themselves into an association; making themselves known as such to the world; appointing him as their agent; and making themselves individually, or as an association, responsible for his acts, done by their authority. Until all this can be shown, no one can say that, in any legitimate sense, there is any such association; or that he is their agent; or that he ever gave his oath *to them;* or ever pledged his faith *to them.*

On general principles of law and reason, it would be a sufficient answer for him to say, to all individuals, and all pretended associations of individuals, who should accuse him of a breach of faith to them:

I never knew you. Where is your evidence that *you,* either individually or collectively, ever appointed me *your* attorney? that *you* ever required me to swear *to you,* that, as *your* attorney, I would support the Constitution? or that I have now broken any faith I ever pledged *to you?* You may, or you may not, be members of that secret band of robbers and murderers, who act in secret; appoint their agents by a secret ballot; who keep themselves *individually* unknown even to the agents they thus appoint; and who, therefore, cannot claim that they have any agents; or that any of their pretended agents ever gave his oath, or pledged his faith, *to them.* I repudiate you altogether. My oath was given to others, with whom you have nothing to do; or it was idle wind, given only to the idle winds. Begone!

XII.

For the same reasons, the oaths of all the other pretended agents of this secret band of robbers and murderers are on general principles of law and reason, equally destitute of obligation. They are given to nobody; but only to the winds.

The oaths of the tax-gatherers and treasurers of the band, are, on general principles of law and reason, of no validity. If any tax gatherer, for example, should put the money he receives into his own pocket, and refuse to part with it, the members of this band could not say to him: You collected that money as *our* agent, and for *our* uses; and you swore to pay it over to *us*, or to those *we* should appoint to receive it. You have betrayed *us*, and broken faith with *us*.

It would be a sufficient answer for him to say to them:

I never knew you. You never made yourselves *individually* known to me. I never gave my oath to you, as individuals. You may, or you may not, be members of that secret band, who appoint agents to rob and murder other people; but who are cautious not to make themselves individually known, either to such agents, or to those whom their agents are commissioned to rob. If you are members of that band, you have given me no proof of it, and you have no proof that you ever commissioned me to rob others for your benefit. I never knew you, as individuals, and of course never promised you that I would pay over to you the proceeds of my robberies. I committed my robberies on my own account, and for my own profit. If you thought I was fool enough to allow you to keep yourselves concealed, and use me as your tool for robbing other persons; or that I would take all the personal risk of the robberies, and pay over the proceeds to you, you were particularly simple. As I took all the risk of my robberies, I propose to take all the profits. Begone! You are fools, as well as villains. If I gave my oath to anybody, I gave it to other persons than you. But I really gave it to nobody. I only gave it to the winds. It answered my purposes at the time. It enabled me to get the money I was after, and now I propose to keep it. If you expected me to pay it over to you, you relied only upon that honor that is said to prevail among thieves. You now understand that that is a very poor reliance. I trust you may become wise enough to never rely upon it again. If I have any *duty* in the matter, it is to give back the money to those from whom I took it; not to pay it over to such villains as you.

48

XIII.

On general principles of law and reason, the oaths which foreigners take, on coming here, and being "naturalized" (as it is called), are of no validity. They are necessarily given to nobody; because there is no open, authentic association, to which they *can* join themselves; or to whom, as individuals, they *can* pledge their faith. No such association, or organization, as "the people of the United States," having ever been formed by any open, written, authentic, or voluntary contract, there is, on general principles of law and reason, no such association, or organization, in existence. And all oaths that purport to be given to such an association are necessarily given only to the winds. They cannot be said to be given to any man, or body of men, as individuals, because no man, or body of men, can come forward *with any proof* that the oaths were given to them, as individuals, or to any association of which they are members. To say that there is a tacit understanding among a portion of the male adults of the country, that they will call themselves "the people of the United States," and that they will act in concert in subjecting the remainder of the people of the United States to their dominion; but that they will keep themselves personally concealed by doing all their acts secretly, is wholly insufficient, on general principles of law and reason, to prove the existence of any such association, or organization, as "the people of the United States;" or consequently to prove that the oaths of foreigners were given to any such association.

XIV.

On general principles of law and reason, all the oaths which, since the war, have been given by Southern men, that they will obey the laws of Congress, support the Union, and the like, are of no validity. Such oaths are invalid, not only because they were extorted by military power, and threats of confiscation, and because they are in contravention of men's natural right to do as they please about supporting the government, *but also because they were given to nobody.* They were nominally given to "the United States." But being nominally given to "the United States," they were necessarily given to nobody, because, on general principles of law and reason, there were no "United States," to whom the oaths could be given. That is to say, there was no open, authentic, avowed, legitimate association, corporation, or body of men, known as "the United States," or as "the people of the United States," to whom the oaths could have been given. If anybody says there was such a corporation, let him state who were the individuals that composed it, and how and when they became a corporation. Were

49

Mr. A, Mr. B, and Mr. C members of it? If so, where are their signatures? Where the evidence of their membership? Where the record? Where the open, authentic proof? There is none. Therefore, in law and reason, there was no such corporation.

On general principles of law and reason, every corporation, association, or organized body of men, having a legitimate corporate existence, and legitimate corporate rights, must consist of certain known individuals, *who can prove, by legitimate and reasonable evidence, their membership.* But nothing of this kind can be proved in regard to the corporation, or body of men, who call themselves "the United States." Not a man of them, in all the Northern States, can prove by any legitimate evidence, such as is required to prove membership in other legal corporations, that he himself, or any other man whom he can name, is a member of any corporation or association called "the United States," or "the people of the United States," or, consequently, that there is any such corporation. And since no such corporation can be proved to exist, it cannot of course be proved that the oaths of Southern men were given to any such corporation. The most that can be claimed is that the oaths were given to a secret band of robbers and murderers, who called themselves "the United States," and extorted those oaths. But that certainly is not enough to prove that the oaths are of any obligation.

XV.

On general principles of law and reason, the oaths of soldiers, that they will serve a given number of years, that they will obey the orders of their superior officers, that they will bear true allegiance to the government, and so forth, are of no obligation. Independently of the criminality of an oath, that, for a given number of years, he will kill all whom he may be commanded to kill, without exercising his own judgment or conscience as to the justice or necessity of such killing, there is this further reason why a soldier's oath is of no obligation, viz. that, like all the other oaths that have now been mentioned, *it is given to nobody.* There being, in no legitimate sense, any such corporation, or nation, as "the United States," nor, consequently, in any legitimate sense, any such government as "the government of the United States," a soldier's oath given to, or contract made with, such nation or government, is necessarily an oath given to, or a contract made with, nobody. Consequently such oath or contract can be of no obligation.

XVI.

On general principles of law and reason, the treaties, so called, which purport to be entered into with other nations, by certain persons calling themselves ambassadors, secretaries, presidents, and senators of the United States, in the name, and on behalf, of "the people of the United States," are of no validity. These so-called ambassadors, secretaries, presidents, and senators, who claim to be the agents of "the people of the United States," for making these treaties, can show no open, written, or other authentic evidence that either the whole "people of the United States," or any other open, avowed, responsible body of men, calling themselves by that name, ever authorized these pretended ambassadors and others to make treaties in the name of, or binding upon any one of, "the people of the United States." Neither can they show any open, written, or other authentic evidence that either the whole "people of the United States," or any other open, avowed, responsible body of men, calling themselves by that name, ever authorized these pretended ambassadors, secretaries, and others, in their name and behalf, to recognize certain other persons, calling themselves emperors, kings, queens, and the like, as the rightful rulers, sovereigns, masters, or representatives of the different peoples whom they assume to govern, to represent, and to bind.

The "nations," as they are called, with whom our pretended ambassadors, secretaries, presidents and senators profess to make treaties, are as much myths as our own. On general principles of law and reason, there are no such "nations." That is to say, neither the whole people of England, for example, nor any open, avowed, responsible body of men, calling themselves by that name, ever, by any open, written, or other authentic contract with each other, formed themselves into any *bona fide,* legitimate association or organization, or authorized any king, queen, or other representative to make treaties in their name, or to bind them, either individually, or as an association, by such treaties.

Our pretended treaties, then, being made with no legitimate or *bona fide* nations, or representatives of nations, and being made, on our part, by persons who have no legitimate authority to act for us, have intrinsically no more validity than a pretended treaty made by the Man in the Moon with the king of the Pleiades.

XVII.

On general principles of law and reason, debts contracted in the name of "the United States," or of "the people of the United States," are of no validity. It is utterly absurd to pretend that debts to the amount of twenty-five hundred millions of dollars are binding upon thirty-five or forty millions of people, when there is not a particle of legitimate evidence—such as would be required to prove a private debt—that can be produced against any one of them, that either he, or his properly authorized attorney, ever contracted to pay one cent.

Certainly, neither the whole people of the United States, nor any number of them, ever separately or individually contracted to pay a cent of these debts.

Certainly, also, neither the whole people of the United States, nor any number of them, ever, by any open, written, or other authentic and voluntary contract, united themselves as a firm, corporation, or association, by the name of "the United States," or "the people of the United States," and authorized their agents to contract debts in their name.

Certainly, too, there is in existence no such firm, corporation, or association as "the United States," or "the people of the United States," formed by any open, written, or other authentic and voluntary contract, and having corporate property with which to pay these debts.

How, then, is it possible, on any general principle of law or reason, that debts that are binding upon nobody individually, can be binding upon forty millions of people collectively, when, on general and legitimate principles of law and reason, these forty millions of people neither have, nor ever had, any corporate property? never made any corporate or individual contract? and neither have, nor ever had, any corporate existence?

Who, then, created these debts, in the name of "the United States?" Why, at most, only a few persons, calling themselves "members of Congress," &c. who pretended to represent "the people of the United States," but who really represented only a secret band of robbers and murderers, who wanted money to carry on the robberies and murders in which they were then engaged; and who intended to extort from the future people of the United States, by robbery and threats of murder (and real murder, if that should prove necessary), the means to pay these debts.

This band of robbers and murderers, who were the real principals in contracting these debts, is a secret one, because its members have never entered into any open, written, avowed, or authentic contract, by which they may be individually known to the world, or even to each other. Their real or pretended representatives, who contracted these debts in their name, were selected (if selected at all) for that purpose secretly (by secret ballot), and in a way to furnish evidence against none of the principals *individually;* and these principals were really known *individually* neither to their pretended representatives who contracted these debts in their behalf, nor to those who lent the money. The money, therefore, was all borrowed and lent in the dark; that is, by men who did not see each other's faces, or know each other's names; who could not then, and cannot now, identify each other as principals in the transactions; and who consequently can prove no contract with each other.

Furthermore, the money was all lent and borrowed for criminal purposes; that is, for purposes of robbery and murder; and for this reason the contracts were all intrinsically void; and would have been so, even though the real parties, borrowers and lenders, had come face to face, and made their contracts openly, in their own proper names.

Furthermore, this secret band of robbers and murderers, who were the real borrowers of this money, having no legitimate corporate existence, have no corporate property with which to pay these debts. They do indeed pretend to own large tracts of wild lands, lying between the Atlantic and Pacific Oceans, and between the Gulf of Mexico and the North Pole. But, on general principles of law and reason, they might as well pretend to own the Atlantic and Pacific Oceans themselves; or the atmosphere and the sunlight; and to hold them, and dispose of them, for the payment of these debts.

Having no corporate property with which to pay what purports to be their corporate debts, this secret band of robbers and murderers are really bankrupt. They have nothing to pay with. In fact, they do not propose to pay their debts otherwise than from the proceeds of their future robberies and murders. These are confessedly their sole reliance; and were known to be such by the lenders of the money, at the time the money was lent. And it was, therefore, virtually a part of the contract, that the money should be repaid only from the proceeds of these future robberies and murders. For this reason, if for no other, the contracts were void from the beginning.

In fact, these apparently two classes, borrowers and lenders, were really one and the same class. They borrowed and lent money from and to themselves. They themselves were not only part and parcel, but the very life and soul, of this secret band of robbers and murderers, who borrowed and spent the money. Individually they furnished money for a common enterprise; taking, in return, what purported to be corporate

53

promises for individual loans. The only excuse they had for taking these so-called corporate promises of, for individual loans by, the same parties, was that they might have some apparent excuse for the future robberies of the band (that is, to pay the debts of the corporation), and that they might also know what shares they were to be respectively entitled to out of the proceeds of their future robberies.

Finally, if these debts had been created for the most innocent and honest purposes, and in the most open and honest manner, by the real parties to the contracts, these parties could thereby have bound nobody but themselves, and no property but their own. They could have bound nobody that should have come after them, and no property subsequently created by, or belonging to, other persons.

XVIII.

The Constitution having never been signed by anybody; and there being no other open, written, or authentic contract between any parties whatever, by virtue of which the United States government, so called, is maintained; and it being well known that none but male persons, of twenty-one years of age and upwards, are allowed any voice in the government; and it being also well known that a large number of these adult persons seldom or never vote at all; and that *all* those who do vote, do so secretly (by secret ballot), and in a way to prevent their individual votes being known, either to the world, or even to each other; and consequently in a way to make no one openly responsible for the acts of their agents, or representatives,—all these things being known, the questions arise: *Who* compose the real governing power in the country? Who are the men, *the responsible men,* who rob us of our property? Restrain us of our liberty? Subject us to their arbitrary dominion? And devastate our homes, and shoot us down by the hundreds of thousands, if we resist? How shall we find these men? How shall we know them from others? How shall we defend ourselves and our property against them? Who, of our neighbors, are members of this secret band of robbers and murderers? How can we know which are *their* houses, that we may burn or demolish them? Which *their* property, that we may destroy it? Which *their* persons, that we may kill them, and rid the world and ourselves of such tyrants and monsters?

These are questions that must be answered, before men can be free; before they can protect themselves against this secret band of robbers and murderers, who now plunder, enslave, and destroy them.

The answer to these questions is, that only those who have the will and the power to shoot down their fellow men, are the real rulers in this, as in all other (so called) civilized countries; for by no others will civilized men be robbed, or enslaved.

Among savages, mere physical strength, on the part of one man, may enable him to rob, enslave, or kill another man. Among barbarians, mere physical strength, on the part of a body of men, disciplined, and acting in concert, though with very little money or other wealth, may, under some circumstances, enable them to rob, enslave, or kill another body of men, as numerous, or perhaps even more numerous, than themselves. And among both savages and barbarians, mere want may sometimes compel one man to sell himself as a slave to another. But with (so called) civilized peoples, among whom knowledge, wealth, and the means of acting in concert, have become diffused; and who have invented such weapons and other means of defence as to render mere physical strength of less importance; and by whom soldiers in any requisite number, and other instrumentalities of war in any requisite amount, can always be had for money, the question of war, and consequently the question of power, is little else than a mere question of money. As a necessary consequence, those who stand ready to furnish this money, are the real rulers. It is so in Europe, and it is so in this country.

In Europe, the nominal rulers, the emperors and kings and parliaments, are anything but the real rulers of their respective countries. They are little or nothing else than mere tools, employed by the wealthy to rob, enslave, and (if need be) murder those who have less wealth, or none at all.

The Rothschilds, and that class of money-lenders of whom they are the representatives and agents,—men who never think of lending a shilling to their next-door neighbors, for purposes of honest industry, unless upon the most ample security, and at the highest rate of interest,— stand ready, at all times, to lend money in unlimited amounts to those robbers and murderers, who call themselves governments, to be expended in shooting down those who do not submit quietly to being robbed and enslaved.

They lend their money in this manner, knowing that it is to be expended in murdering their fellow men, for simply seeking their liberty and their rights; knowing also that neither the interest nor the principal will ever be paid, except as it will be extorted under terror of the repetition of such murders as those for which the money lent is to be expended.

These money-lenders, the Rothschilds, for example, say to themselves: If we lend a hundred millions sterling to the Queen and Parliament of England, it will enable them to murder twenty, fifty, or a hundred thousand people in England, Ireland, or India; and the terror inspired by such wholesale murder, will enable them to keep the whole people of those countries in subjection for twenty, or perhaps fifty, years to come; to control all their trade and industry; and to extort from them large amounts of money, under the name of taxes; and from the wealth thus extorted from them, they (the Queen and Parliament) can afford to pay us a higher rate of interest for our money than we can get in any other way. Or, if we lend this sum to the Emperor of Austria, it will enable him to murder so many of his people as to strike terror into the rest, and thus enable him to keep them in subjection, and extort money from them, for twenty or fifty years to come. And they say the same in regard to the Emperor of Russia, the King of Prussia, the Emperor of France, or any other ruler, so called, who, in their judgment, will be able, by murdering a reasonable portion of his people, to keep the rest in subjection, and extort money from them, for a long time to come, to pay the interest and principal of the money lent him.

And why are these men so ready to lend money for murdering their fellow men? Solely for this reason, viz., that such loans are considered better investments than loans for purposes of honest industry. They pay higher rates of interest; and it is less trouble to look after them. This is the whole matter.

The question of making these loans is, with these lenders, a mere question of pecuniary profit. They lend money to be expended in robbing, enslaving, and murdering their fellow men, solely because, on the whole, such loans pay better than any others. They are no respecters of persons, no superstitious fools, that reverence monarchs. They care no more for a king, or an emperor, than they do for a beggar, except as he is a better customer, and can pay them better interest for their money. If they doubt his ability to make his murders successful for maintaining his power, and thus extorting money from his people in future, they dismiss him as unceremoniously as they would dismiss any other hopeless bankrupt, who should want to borrow money to save himself from open insolvency.

When these great lenders of blood-money, like the Rothschilds, have loaned vast sums in this way, for purposes of murder, to an emperor or a king, they sell out the bonds taken by them, in small amounts, to anybody, and everybody, who are disposed to buy them at satisfactory prices, to hold as investments. They (the Rothschilds) thus soon get back their money, with great profits; and are now ready to lend money in the same way again to any other robber and murderer, called an emperor or a king, who, they think, is likely to be successful in his robberies and murders, and able to pay a good price for the money necessary to carry them on.

This business of lending blood-money is one of the most thoroughly sordid, cold-blooded and criminal that was ever carried on, to any considerable extent, amongst human beings. It is like lending money to slave-traders, or to common robbers and pirates, to be repaid out of their plunder. And the men who loan money to governments, so called, for the purpose of enabling the latter to rob, enslave, and murder their people, are among the greatest villains that the world has ever seen. And they as much deserve to be hunted and killed (if they cannot otherwise be got rid of) as any slave-traders, robbers, or pirates that ever lived.

When these emperors and kings, so called, have obtained their loans, they proceed to hire and train immense numbers of professional murderers, called soldiers, and employ them in shooting down all who resist their demands for money. In fact, most of them keep large bodies of these murderers constantly in their service, as their only means of enforcing their extortions. There are now, I think, four or five millions of these professional murderers constantly employed by the so-called sovereigns of Europe. The enslaved people are, of course, forced to support and pay all these murderers, as well as to submit to all the other extortions which these murderers are employed to enforce.

It is only in this way that most of the so-called governments of Europe are maintained. These so-called governments are in reality only great bands of robbers and murderers, organized, disciplined, and constantly on the alert. And the so-called sovereigns, in these different governments, are simply the heads, or chiefs, of different bands of robbers and murderers. And these heads or chiefs are dependent upon the lenders of blood-money for the means to carry on their robberies and murders. They could not sustain themselves a moment but for the loans made to them by these blood-money loan-mongers. And their first care is to maintain their credit with them; for they know their end is come, the instant their credit with them fails. Consequently the first proceeds of their extortions are scrupulously applied to the payment of the interest on their loans.

In addition to paying the interest on their bonds, they perhaps grant to the holders of them great monopolies in banking, like the Banks of

England, of France, and of Vienna; with the agreement that these banks shall furnish money whenever, in sudden emergencies, it may be necessary to shoot down more of their people. Perhaps also, by means of tariffs on competing imports, they give great monopolies to certain branches of industry, in which these lenders of blood-money are engaged. They also, by unequal taxation, exempt wholly or partially the property of these loan-mongers, and throw corresponding burdens upon those who are too poor and weak to resist.

Thus it is evident that all these men, who call themselves by the high-sounding names of Emperors, Kings, Sovereigns, Monarchs, Most Christian Majesties, Most Catholic Majesties, High Mightinesses, Most Serene and Potent Princes, and the like, and who claim to rule "by the grace of God," by "Divine Right,"—that is, by special authority from Heaven,—are intrinsically not only the merest miscreants and wretches, engaged solely in plundering, enslaving, and murdering their fellow men, but that they are also the merest hangers on, the servile, obsequious, fawning dependents and tools of these blood-money loan-mongers, on whom they rely for the means to carry on their crimes. These loan-mongers, like the Rothschilds, laugh in their sleeves, and say to themselves: These despicable creatures, who call themselves emperors, and kings, and majesties, and most serene and potent princes; who profess to wear crowns, and sit on thrones; who deck themselves with ribbons, and feathers, and jewels; and surround themselves with hired flatterers and lickspittles; and whom we suffer to strut around, and palm themselves off, upon fools and slaves, as sovereigns and lawgivers specially appointed by Almighty God; and to hold themselves out as the sole fountains of honors, and dignities, and wealth, and power,—all these miscreants and impostors know that we make them, and use them; that in us they live, move, and have their being; that we require them (as the price of their positions) to take upon themselves all the labor, all the danger, and all the odium of all the crimes they commit for our profit; and that we will unmake them, strip them of their gewgaws, and send them out into the world as beggars, or give them over to the vengeance of the people they have enslaved, the moment they refuse to commit any crime we require of them, or to pay over to us such share of the proceeds of their robberies as we see fit to demand.

XIX.

Now, what is true in Europe, is substantially true in this country. The difference is the immaterial one, that, in this country, there is no visible, *permanent* head, or chief, of these robbers and murderers, who call themselves "the government." That is to say, there is no *one man,* who calls himself the state, or even emperor, king, or sovereign; no one who claims that he and his children rule "by the Grace of God," by "Divine Right," or by special appointment from Heaven. There are only certain men, who call themselves presidents, senators, and representatives, and claim to be the authorized agents, *for the time being, or for certain short periods,* of *all* "the people of the United States;" but who can show no credentials, or powers of attorney, or any other open, authentic evidence that they are so; and who notoriously are not so; but are really only the agents of a secret band of robbers and murderers, whom they themselves do not know, and have no means of knowing, individually; but who, they trust, will openly or secretly, when the crisis comes, sustain them in all their usurpations and crimes.

What is important to be noticed is, that these so-called presidents, senators, and representatives, these pretended agents of *all* "the people of the United States," the moment their exactions meet with any formidable resistance from any portion of "the people" themselves, are obliged, like their co-robbers and murderers in Europe, to fly at once to the lenders of blood money, for the means to sustain their power. And they borrow their money on the same principle, and for the same purpose, viz., to be expended in shooting down all those "people of the United States"—their own constituents and principals, as they profess to call them—who resist the robberies and enslavement which these borrowers of the money are practising upon them. And they expect to repay the loans, if at all, only from the proceeds of the future robberies, which they anticipate it will be easy for them and their successors to perpetrate through a long series of years, upon their pretended principals, if they can but shoot down *now* some hundreds of thousands of them, and thus strike terror into the rest.

Perhaps the facts were never made more evident, in any country on the globe, than in our own, that these soulless blood-money loan-mongers are the real rulers; that they rule from the most sordid and mercenary motives; that the ostensible government, the presidents, senators, and representatives, so-called, are merely their tools; and that no ideas of, or regard for, justice or liberty had anything to do in inducing them to lend their money for the war. In proof of all this, look at the following facts.

Nearly a hundred years ago we professed to have got rid of all that religious superstition, inculcated by a servile and corrupt priesthood in

Europe, that rulers, so called, derived their authority directly from Heaven; and that it was consequently a religious duty on the part of the people to obey them. We professed long ago to have learned that governments could rightfully exist only by the free will, and on the voluntary support, of those who might choose to sustain them. We all professed to have known long ago, that the only legitimate objects of government were the maintenance of liberty and justice equally for all. All this we had professed for nearly a hundred years. And we professed to look with pity and contempt upon those ignorant, superstitious, and enslaved peoples of Europe, who were so easily kept in subjection by the frauds and force of priests and kings.

Notwithstanding all this, that we had learned, and known, and professed, for nearly a century, these lenders of blood money had, for a long series of years previous to the war, been the willing accomplices of the slave-holders in perverting the government from the purposes of liberty and justice, to the greatest of crimes. They had been such accomplices *for a purely pecuniary consideration,* to wit, a control of the markets in the South; in other words, the privilege of holding the slave-holders them-selves in industrial and commercial subjection to the manufacturers and merchants of the North (who afterwards furnished the money for the war). And these Northern merchants and manufacturers, these lenders of blood-money, were willing to continue to be the accomplices of the slave-holders in the future, for the same pecuniary consideration. But the slave-holders, either doubting the fidelity of their Northern allies, or feeling themselves strong enough to keep their slaves in subjection without Northern assistance, would no longer pay the price which these Northern men demanded. And it was to enforce this price in the future—that is, to monopolize the Southern markets, to maintain their industrial and commercial control over the South—that these Northern manufacturers and merchants lent some of the profits of their former monopolies for the war, in order to secure to themselves the same, or greater, monopolies in the future. These—and not any love of liberty or justice—were the motives on which the money for the war was lent by the North. In short, the North said to the slave-holders: If you will not pay us our price (give us control of your markets) for our assistance against your slaves, we will secure the same price (keep control of your markets) by helping your slaves against you, and using them as our tools for maintaining dominion over you; for the control of your markets we will have, whether the tools we use for that purpose be black or white, and be the cost, in blood and money, what it may.

On this principle, and from this motive, and not from any love of liberty or justice, the money was lent in enormous amounts, and at enormous rates of interest. And it was only by means of these loans that the objects of the war were accomplished.

And now these lenders of blood-money demand their pay; and the government, so called, becomes their tool, their servile, slavish, villanous tool, to extort it from the labor of the enslaved people both of the North and the South. It is to be extorted by every form of direct, and indirect, and unequal taxation. Not only the nominal debt and interest—enormous as the latter was—are to be paid in full; but these holders of the debt are to be paid still further—and perhaps doubly, triply, or quadruply paid—by such tariffs on imports as will enable our home manufacturers to realize enormous prices for their commodities; also by such monopolies in banking as will enable them to keep control of, and thus enslave and plunder, the industry and trade of the great body of the Northern people themselves. In short, the industrial and commercial slavery of the great body of the people, North and South, black and white, is the price which these-lenders of blood money demand, and insist upon, and are determined to secure, in return for the money lent for the war.

This programme having been fully arranged and systematized, they put their sword into the hands of the chief murderer of the war, and charge him to carry their scheme into effect. And now he, speaking as their organ, says: "*Let us have peace.*"

The meaning of this is: Submit quietly to all the robbery and slavery we have arranged for you, and you can have "peace." But in case you resist, the same lenders of blood-money, who furnished the means to subdue the South, will furnish the means again to subdue you.

These are the terms on which alone this government, or, with few exceptions, any other, ever gives "peace" to its people.

The whole affair, on the part of those who furnished the money, has been, and now is, a deliberate scheme of robbery and murder; not merely to monopolize the markets of the South, but also to monopolize the currency, and thus control the industry and trade, and thus plunder and enslave the laborers, of both North and South. And Congress and the president are to-day the merest tools for these purposes. They are obliged to be, for they know that their own power, as rulers, so called, is at an end, the moment their credit with the blood-money loan-mongers fails. They are like a bankrupt in the hands of an extortioner.

They dare not say nay to any demand made upon them. And to hide at once, if possible, both their servility and their crimes, they attempt to divert public attention, by crying out that they have "Abolished Slavery!" That they have "Saved the Country!" That they have "Preserved our Glorious Union!" and that, in now paying the "National Debt," as they call it (as if the people themselves, *all of them who are to be taxed for its payment,* had really and voluntarily joined in contracting it), they are simply "Maintaining the National Honor!"

By "maintaining the national honor," they mean simply that they themselves, open robbers and murderers, assume to be the nation, and will keep faith with those who lend them the money necessary to enable them to crush the great body of the people under their feet; and will faithfully appropriate, from the proceeds of their future robberies and murders, enough to pay all their loans, principal and interest.

The pretence that the "abolition of slavery" was either a motive or justification for the war, is a fraud of the same character with that of "maintaining the national honor." Who, but such usurpers, robbers, and murderers as they, ever established slavery? Or what government, except one resting upon the sword, like the one we now have, was ever capable of maintaining slavery? And why did these men abolish slavery? Not from any love of liberty in general—not as an act of justice to the black man himself, but only "as a war measure," and because they wanted his assistance, and that of his friends, in carrying on the war they had undertaken for maintaining and intensifying that political, commercial, and industrial slavery, to which they have subjected the great body of the people, both white and black. And yet these impostors now cry out that they have abolished the chattel slavery of the black man—although that was not the motive of the war—as if they thought they could thereby conceal, atone for, or justify that other slavery which they were fighting to perpetuate, and to render more rigorous and inexorable than it ever was before. There was no difference of principle—but only of degree—between the slavery they boast they have abolished, and the slavery they were fighting to preserve; for all restraints upon men's natural liberty, not necessary for the simple maintenance of justice, are of the nature of slavery, and differ from each other only in degree.

If their object had really been to abolish slavery, or maintain liberty or justice generally, they had only to say: All, whether white or black, who want the protection of this government, shall have it; and all who do not want it, will be left in peace, so long as they leave us in peace. Had they said this, slavery would necessarily have been abolished at once; the war would have been saved; and a thousand times nobler union than we have ever had would have been the result. It would have been a voluntary union of free men; such a union as will one day exist among all men, the world over, if the several nations, so called, shall ever get rid of the usurpers, robbers, and murderers, called governments, that now plunder, enslave, and destroy them.

Still another of the frauds of these men is, that they are now establishing, and that the war was designed to establish, "a government of consent." The only idea they have ever manifested as to what is a government of consent, is this—that it is one to which everybody must consent, or be shot. This idea was the dominant one on which the war was carried on; and it is the dominant one, now that we have got what is called "peace."

Their pretences that they have "Saved the Country," and "Preserved our Glorious Union," are frauds like all the rest of their pretences. By them they mean simply that they have subjugated, and maintained their power over, an unwilling people. This they call "Saving the Country;" as if an enslaved and subjugated people—or as if any people kept in subjection by the sword (as it is intended that all of us shall be hereafter)—could be said to have any country. This, too, they call "Preserving our Glorious Union;" as if there could be said to be any Union, glorious or inglorious, that was not voluntary. Or as if there could be said to be any union between masters and slaves; between those who conquer, and those who are subjugated.

All these cries of having "abolished slavery," of having "saved the country," of having "preserved the union," of establishing "a government of consent," and of "maintaining the national honor," are all gross, shameless, transparent cheats—so transparent that they ought to deceive no one—when uttered as justifications for the war, or for the government that has succeeded the war, or for now compelling the people to pay the cost of the war, or for compelling anybody to support a government that he does not want.

The lesson taught by all these facts is this: As long as mankind continue to pay "National Debts," so-called,—that is, so long as they are such dupes and cowards as to pay for being cheated, plundered, enslaved, and murdered,—so long there will be enough to lend the money for those purposes; and with that money a plenty of tools, called soldiers, can be hired to keep them in subjection. But when they refuse any longer to pay for being thus cheated, plundered, enslaved, and murdered, they will cease to have cheats, and usurpers, and robbers, and murderers and blood-money loan-mongers for masters.

Appendix.

Inasmuch as the Constitution was never signed, nor agreed to, by anybody, as a contract, and therefore never bound anybody, and is now binding upon nobody; and is, moreover, such an one as no people can ever hereafter be expected to consent to, except as they may be forced to do so at the point of the bayonet, it is perhaps of no importance what its true legal meaning, as a contract, is. Nevertheless, the writer thinks it proper to say that, in his opinion, the Constitution is no such instrument as it has generally been assumed to be; but that by false interpretations, and naked usurpations, the government has been made in practice a very widely, and almost wholly, different thing from what the Constitution itself purports to authorize. He has heretofore written much, and could write much more, to prove that such is the truth. But whether the Constitution really be one thing, or another, this much is certain—that it has either authorized such a government as we have had, or has been powerless to prevent it. In either case, it is unfit to exist.

Made in United States
North Haven, CT
13 April 2022

18234724R00039